SCOTT FORESMAN ENGLISH

ON TARGET 1

INTERMEDIATE

Second Edition

James E. Purpura
Teachers College, Columbia University

Diane Pinkley
Teachers College, Columbia University

On Target 1, Second Edition

Pearson Education, 10 Bank Street, White Plains, NY 10606

Editorial directors: Allen Ascher and Louise Jennewine
Acquisitions editor: Bill Preston
Director of design and production: Rhea Banker
Development editor: Laura Le Dréan
Production manager: Alana Zdinak
Production supervisor: Liza Pleva
Managing editor: Linda Moser
Senior production editor: Virginia Bernard
Senior manufacturing manager: Patrice Fraccio
Manufacturing supervisor: Edith Pullman
Photo research: Quarasan and Aerin Csigay
Cover design: Charles Yuen
Text design and composition: Quarasan
Photo and illustration credits: See p.vi.

Library of Congress Cataloging-in-Publication Data
Purpura, James E. (James Enos),
  On Target 1: intermediate / James E. Purpura, Diane Pinkley.—2nd ed.
    p. cm.—(Scott Foresman English)
  Includes index.
  ISBN 0-201-57978-2
  1. English language textbooks for foreign speakers. I. Pinkley, Diane. II. Title.
III. Title: On Target 1. IV Series.

PE1128.P87 1999
428.2'4—dc21

                                    99-36749
                                        CIP

ISBN: 0-201-57978-2
1 2 3 4 5 6 7 8 9 10—PO—04 03 02 01 00 99

CONTENTS

SUMMARY OF SKILLS

Theme	Grammar	Listening and Speaking	Reading and Writing
Unit 1 **What's on TV?** Page 1	Simple Present Tense; Future Events Frequency Adverbs and Expressions	**Listening:** Coming Soon! ➡ Listening for Specific Details **Pronunciation:** -s/-es ending **Speaking:** What's Your Opinion? ➡ Expressing Opinions	**Reading:** TV Programs ➡ Scanning **Writing:** The Paragraph
Unit 2 **People Watching** Page 11	Present Progressive Tense: Present Time; Future Time Stative Verbs	**Listening:** Where Are They? ➡ Making Inferences **Pronunciation:** Syllables **Speaking:** The Meeting ➡ Making Appointments	**Reading:** The Right to Privacy ➡ Guessing Meaning from Context **Writing:** Narrowing a Topic
Unit 3 **Keeping Up with the Joneses** Page 21	Comparative Adjectives; *Not as ... as;* Talking about Similarities	**Listening:** Choosing a Restaurant ➡ Listening for Criteria **Pronunciation:** Stressed Syllables **Speaking:** Alternatives ➡ Agreeing and Disagreeing	**Reading:** Mall Crawlers: A Teenage Stereotype ➡ Identifying Main Ideas **Writing:** The Topic Sentence

Review (Units 1–3)

Theme	Grammar	Listening and Speaking	Reading and Writing
Unit 4 **And the Beat Goes On!** Page 33	Simple Past Tense; Adverbs of Sequence	**Listening:** Music Around the World ➡ Listening to Complete a Chart **Pronunciation:** -ed ending **Speaking:** First-Time Experiences ➡ Keeping a Conversation Going	**Reading:** The Story of Jazz ➡ Noticing Chronological Order **Writing:** Supporting Sentences
Unit 5 **Close Calls** Page 43	Simple Past and Past Progressive Tenses; Time Clauses with *When, While, As*	**Listening:** A News Story ➡ Listening for Sequence **Pronunciation:** Content vs. Function Words **Speaking:** A Close Call ➡ Telling a Story	**Reading:** The San Francisco Earthquake of 1906 ➡ Making Predictions **Writing:** The Concluding Sentence
Unit 6 **The Best in Life** Page 53	Superlative; Making Comparisons with Adverbs and Nouns	**Listening:** Advertisements ➡ Listening to Draw Conclusions **Pronunciation:** Numbers **Speaking:** Five Thousand Dollars ➡ Arguing, Counterarguing, Conceding	**Reading:** The World of Advertising ➡ Noticing Examples **Writing:** Ordering Supporting Sentences

Review (Units 4–6)

Language is communication. In this class, you will communicate in English. You will talk about your ideas, feelings, experiences, and culture. Begin the class by getting to know the other students and the teacher.

Getting Acquainted

1 When you get acquainted with people, you find out information about them. What questions do you ask when you are getting acquainted with someone? Look at the categories. Write an information question for each category. Use the question words from the box for help.

Question Words	
who	where
what	what kind of
how	how often
why	which
when	how long
how many	how much

Categories	Questions
a. name	*What's your name?*
b. hometown or country	
c. job/school	
d. education	
e. reason for studying English	
f. family	
g. hobbies	
h. favorite food	
i. favorite actor/actress	
j. favorite restaurant	
k. favorite weekend activity	
l. other information	

2 Find a partner and get acquainted. Ask each other your questions. Write your partner's answers on a sheet of paper.

3 Introduce your partner to the class.

Getting Down to Business

4 When you are ready to begin work, you "get down to business." In a new class, you ask questions about the course. Look at the class information chart. Use question words to ask your teacher about your course. Write your teacher's answers in the chart.

Class Information	
a. number of units to finish	
b. number of exams	
c. date of final exam	
d. homework	
e. number of compositions	
f. grading	
g. attendance	
h. other information	

What Do You Say?

5 What would you say in each situation? Write the letter of the appropriate expression next to the situation. You can use a letter more than once.

Situation

_____ **1.** You don't know the meaning of a word.

_____ **2.** You don't know a word in English. You know it in your language.

_____ **3.** You didn't hear something.

_____ **4.** You don't understand something in English. You want your teacher to explain it to you.

_____ **5.** You are trying to say something in English, but you are not sure if it's correct.

_____ **6.** People in your culture do something differently than in another culture.

_____ **7.** You want to write a word. You can't write it correctly.

_____ **8.** A classmate says something. You have the same opinion.

_____ **9.** A classmate says something. You have a different opinion.

_____ **10.** You know that two things aren't the same. You want to know why they aren't the same.

Language Expressions

a. Well, in my country, _____.

b. Is it possible to say _____ in English?

c. How do you spell _____?

d. Oh, I don't know. In my opinion, _____.

e. What does _____ mean?

f. Excuse me, I need some help.

g. How do you say _____ in English?

h. What's the difference between _____ and _____?

i. Could you repeat that, please?

j. I agree with you.

WHAT'S ON TV?

GETTING STARTED

Warm Up

1 TV is a popular form of entertainment. Here are some types of TV programs. Describe each one. Can you add two other types of programs?

talk show | docu-mentary | game show | detective show | soap opera | movie | | |

2 You are going to hear parts of five different TV programs. What channel is each program on? Write the channel number in the box.

☐ *Science Fiction Theater* _____
☐ *The World of Nature* _____
☐ *Women Today* _____
☐ *The $10,000 Test* _____
☐ *Nikki Danger—Police Officer* _____

3 Match the program names above with the correct type of program. Write the answers on the lines.

Figure It Out

4 Some people only want to sit on the couch and watch TV. We call these people "couch potatoes." Are you a couch potato? Check the appropriate boxes in the questionnaire below to find out.

		100% Always	Usually	Often	Sometimes	Seldom	0% Never
a	How long is your TV on every day?	☐	☐	☐	☐	☐	☐
b	How often do you eat while you are watching TV?	☐	☐	☐	☐	☐	☐
c	How often do you watch TV when you have guests?	☐	☐	☐	☐	☐	☐
d	How often do you fall asleep with the TV on?	☐	☐	☐	☐	☐	☐
e	How often do you think about your favorite programs before you plan other activities?	☐	☐	☐	☐	☐	☐
f	How often do you turn on the TV right after you get home from work or school?	☐	☐	☐	☐	☐	☐
g	How often do you watch TV instead of reading, going out with friends, or playing sports?	☐	☐	☐	☐	☐	☐

5 Figure out your total points; then look at the information below.

Always = 5 points   *Often = 3 points*   *Seldom = 1 point*
Usually = 4 points   *Sometimes = 2 points*   *Never = 0 points*

0–11 Points	**12–19 Points**	**20–27 Points**	**28–35 Points**
You're not a couch potato! In fact, you're not even a potato chip. You seldom watch TV. You probably have a love for real life and enjoy many activities. However, remember that there are some good programs on TV. Do you ever watch the news, a good documentary, or a good movie?	You're not a couch potato, but you watch TV sometimes. You probably use your time to participate in sports, hobbies, and other fun activities. Make sure that the TV programs you watch are good ones!	You probably watch TV a little too much. You're going to be a couch potato soon if you're not careful! Think of other ways to spend your time. Visit a friend, go to the movies, or read a book. Learn something new, start playing a sport, or begin a new hobby.	You're a real couch potato! Watch out or you'll become a french fry! You probably almost always watch TV in your free time. You don't have many other interests or activities. You need to find new things to do. Start a hobby! Make new friends! Try turning off the TV once in a while!

6 **Vocabulary Check** The frequency adverbs in column A are from the questionnaire. Match the other frequency adverbs and expressions in column B with the correct adverbs in column A.

Column A
_____ **1.** always
_____ **2.** usually
_____ **3.** often
_____ **4.** sometimes
_____ **5.** seldom
_____ **6.** never

Column B
a. rarely
b. once in a while
c. not at all
d. frequently
e. all the time
f. generally

Talk About It

TV marketing managers often interview people about their TV viewing habits. Look at the dialogue.

Ask about favorite program.

A: What's your favorite TV program?

State favorite program.

B: My favorite program is *Nikki Danger—Police Officer.*

Ask about frequency.

A: How often do you watch it?

Tell frequency.

B: I watch it every week.

7 Look at the categories in the questionnaire. On a sheet of paper, write an interview question for each category.

8 Work with a partner. Interview your partner and write his or her answers in the questionnaire.

9 Discuss your interviews with the class.

a. What is your class's favorite TV program?

b. What is the average number of hours that people watch TV per week?

TV Questionnaire

Categories	Responses
a. Favorite TV program	
b. Hours watching TV per week	
c. Usual time to watch TV	
d. Frequency of watching news	

The Simple Present Tense

We use the simple present tense to talk about actions and states in the present that do not usually change. Look at the different uses.

Present Habits	Marco Jobim **watches** sports on TV every night. He almost always **falls asleep** in front of the TV.
Ideas, Opinions, and Feelings	Marco **doesn't enjoy** soap operas. His wife **thinks** he watches too much TV. She **knows** he is becoming a couch potato.
General Truths and Facts	Teenagers in the United States **watch** about twenty-one hours of TV a week. Cable TV and satellite dishes **give** people many more channels.

 1 **Check Your Understanding** Why do we use the simple present tense? Read the sentences below. Write **H** for habits, **G** for general truths and facts, or **I** for ideas, opinions, and feelings.

_____ **a.** Marco Jobim likes TV very much.

_____ **b.** He turns on the TV as soon as he gets home.

_____ **c.** He always watches music videos.

_____ **d.** His TV gets twelve channels.

_____ **e.** At night he often falls asleep in front of his TV.

_____ **f.** His mother thinks he watches too much TV.

_____ **g.** She believes that a lot of TV is bad for people.

Work with a partner. Compare your answers.

2 Write three sentences of your own. Write one sentence for each use.

3 Look at a partner's sentences. Can you name the use for each sentence?

Hanson, a popular musical group

The Simple Present Tense: Future Events

You can also use the simple present tense to talk about future events with timetables and calendars. Look at the examples.

Future Events	A new talk show **starts** next Monday at 9:00 p.m. The World Cup match **is** on TV tomorrow afternoon at 3:00 p.m. My exams **finish** on Friday.

Talk about future events using the words and phrases below.

Example: The Olympic Games start next week.

Events	Verbs	Future Time Words
a new science fiction movie	start	next week (month, year)
final exams	finish	tomorrow (morning, afternoon, night)
summer classes	is (on)	tonight
the Olympic Games	open	on Friday (Saturday, …)
a documentary on UFOs	close	at 7 p.m.

 Work in groups of three. Take turns describing your TV viewing habits.

Example:
A: I watch the news on TV every night.
B: Not me. I only watch sports and game shows.
C: Me too. My favorite show is *Jackpot Shop*.

Frequency Adverbs and Expressions

We use frequency adverbs and expressions to talk about how often an action happens. We ask questions with *How often* or *ever*.

	Subject	Frequency adverb	Verb phrase
How often do you watch the news?	I	**seldom**	watch the news on TV.
	I	**usually**	read the newspaper.
Do you **ever** get news from the Internet?	I	**sometimes**	do.

	Subject	Verb phrase		Frequency expression
Do you **ever** go to the ballet?	We	go		**twice a year.**
How often do you get that magazine?	I	get	it	**weekly.**
How often does your son watch TV?	He	watches	TV	**every day.**

 Look at the chart above.

   a. Where do frequency adverbs come in a sentence?
   b. Where do frequency expressions come in a sentence?

 Check Your Understanding Circle the words and expressions you can use with the simple present tense. Then write a sentence about yourself in the simple present tense for each word you circled.

seldom	once a year
yesterday	next Friday
every Saturday	last night

8 The Yang family always shares the housework. Mr. Yang, Mrs. Yang, Ann, and Mike do different chores.

a. Look at the word box. Match the verbs on the left with the words on the right to make phrases. Write the phrases on the lines under pictures 1 to 8. The first one is done for you.

b. Work with a partner. Describe the Yang family. Who does the chores? How often? Make sentences in the simple present tense.

Example:

Mrs. Yang often irons the clothes on the weekend.

washes	the food
mows	the car
irons	the plants
fixes	the floor
mops	the dog
cooks	the clothes
feeds	the lawn
waters	the dishes

1.

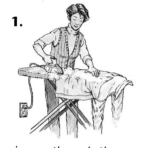

irons the clothes
often/on the weekend

2.

_____
sometimes/on Saturday

3.

_____
always/on weekdays

4.

_____
usually/Saturday morning

5.

_____
normally/every day

6.

_____
generally/twice a week

7.

_____
often/after dinner

8.

_____
usually/Friday evening

9 **Express Yourself** Work with a partner. Who does the chores at your house? How often? Take turns asking and answering questions.

Example:

A: Who usually washes the dishes at your house?

B: I usually do.

A: How often do you wash them?

B: Twice a day.

Unit 1

Listen: Coming Soon!

 Before You Listen

    a. What TV programs can you watch tonight?
    b. What type of program is each one?
    c. What time is each program on?

 Listening for Specific Details We often listen for details such as a name, a date, or a time. We may not understand every word, but we listen for the specific information we need.

Name of Program	Kind of Program	Day	Time
1 *The Big Question*	game show		7:30
2 *Nikki Danger— Police Officer*		Monday	
3		Tuesday	4:00
4 *Spaceship Theater*			8:30
5 *Music City*	music		

  The program *Coming Soon!* is on TV every Sunday. It tells people about next week's programs. Read the chart carefully. Then listen and fill it in.

 Work with a partner. Compare charts and check your answers.

Speak Out

 **Agreeing and Disagreeing** When someone expresses an opinion in a discussion, it is important to know how to agree and disagree politely. Look at the language below.

Agreeing	Disagreeing
Right, I think so too because ...	I'm sorry, but I disagree ...
I don't think so either ...	Well, I'm not sure. I think ...
Yeah, I agree with you because ...	

4 What are your opinions about TV? Read the statements in the chart. Check the boxes.

TV Opinions	I agree	Maybe	I disagree
1. Violent programs make people violent.			
2. Parents need to check the programs their children watch.			
3. Watching TV makes people passive.			
4. You can learn a lot watching TV.			
5. Governments need to control the programs on TV.			

5 Work in groups of three. Share your TV opinions. Use language for agreeing and disagreeing.

Example:

A: I think violent programs make children violent.

B: Well, I'm not sure about that. I watch thrillers all the time and I'm not violent.

C: I don't think so, either.

Pronunciation

The –s/–es ending

In English, we pronounce the –s/–es ending of simple present tense verbs in three ways. The pronunciation depends on the final sound of the verb.

/s/ as in li<u>k</u>es   /z/ as in fa<u>ll</u>s   /ɪz/ as in wa<u>tch</u>es

  6 Listen to the verbs. Do you hear /s/, /z/, or /ɪz/? Write the verbs in the correct boxes below.

/s/ as in *likes*	/z/ as in *falls*	/ɪz/ as in *watches*

 7 Work with a partner. Look at the pictures on page 6 again. Ask and answer questions about the Yang family, using the example. Pay special attention to your pronunciation of –s and –es.

Example:

A: Who mop<u>s</u> the floor?

B: Mike Yang usually mop<u>s</u> it.

READING and WRITING

Read About It

 1 **Before You Read** Predict the kinds of information you could find in a television guide. Circle the letters:

a. program names   **d.** main actors   **g.** program costs
b. program writers   **e.** program types   **h.** program descriptions
c. program times   **f.** number of commercials **i.** channel numbers

 Scanning When you read, you often want to find a fact—a name, a date, a price—quickly. You look for the fact and do not read every word. This kind of reading is called scanning.

2 Scan the program guide. How many of your predictions from Exercise 1 were correct?

3 Scan the program guide again to find the answers to these questions:

   a. How many channels show the news at 6:00 p.m.?

   b. What's on channel 10 at 7:00 p.m.?

   c. What kind of program is *The First Cartoons*?

   d. On which program can you win $20 million?

   e. On which channel can you see a tennis match?

   f. What kind of show is *Z Files*?

   g. How many documentaries are in the program guide?

   h. Who does Ken Cleveland interview?

Think About It

4 Look at the program guide. Which programs would these people like?

- a businessman
- an eleven-year-old girl
- a mother of a small child
- a teenage boy

5 Imagine you own a TV station. With a partner, describe three programs you would like to show on your channel. When you finish, join another pair of students. Describe your programs. Which program do you like best?

TV Programs

6:00

6 21 NEWS

7 OK FOR KIDS *Talk Show.* Children discuss latest kids' movies.

19 $20 MILLION PRIZE *Game Show*

53 The New Doctors *(1984) Movie* George Mendel and Judy Grant are doctors in love in a big-city hospital.

55 24 HOURS *Talk Show* Opera Winfield interviews the first woman in space, Valentina Tereshkova. She describes her work on Space Station Venus.

6:30

2 7 10 NEWS

6 A DAY IN MY LIFE *Comedy* Lance asks Betty to marry him. He gives her a week to decide.

19 MONEY TALK *Talk Show* David Montoya, President of City Bank, discusses the high cost of living. He describes ways to save money.

37 SPORTS WORLD *Tennis* Live from Wimbledon, England

39 THE FIRST CAR-TOONS *Documentary* Paul Dismay tells stories of early cartoons.

55 CHINESE CHEF *Cooking* The chef explains how to cook Szechwan chicken and fried bananas.

7:00

2 NINETY MINUTES *Documentary* Mike Walters reports on teen-age couch potatoes. He explains how to stop watching TV.

6 LIVING TODAY *Documentary* A Mexican teenager describes his first parachute jump.

7 The Return of King Kong (1989) *Movie* King Kong returns to New York. He climbs the World Trade Center this time.

10 THE RICH AND THE FAMOUS *Talk Show* Ken Cleveland interviews singer Gloria Esteban. He visits her one hundred-room mansion.

19 Z FILES *Science Fiction* A doctor thinks his new neighbors are aliens. He asks Mouldy and Smelly to find out.

31 FIX IT YOURSELF *Home Repair* Jack and Julie explain how to fix a broken window.

Write: What Is a Paragraph?

A paragraph is a group of sentences that develops one main idea. In a well-written paragraph, all the sentences are about this one main idea. The first sentence in a paragraph is generally indented from the left-hand margin.

 Here are two paragraphs. Read them and answer the questions below.

Paragraph A

    My favorite TV program is *60 Minutes*. It usually has three different stories about people or events in the news. Frequently, there is an interview with a musician, singer, or other famous person in politics, sports, business, or the arts. Sometimes the stories are about ordinary people who do something special or unusual. *60 Minutes* has excellent reporters and a variety of interesting stories on many topics. I always learn something new from *60 Minutes*, so I try to watch it every week.

Paragraph B

My favorite TV program is *Cinema 13*. *Cinema 13* is on every Saturday night at 9:00 on channel 13. Every week, they show a different movie. I like old movies, especially movies from different countries. You can learn many things about different countries by watching movies. I really like Japanese and French movies. My favorite Japanese film is *Rashomon*, directed by Akira Kurosawa. *Channel 13* is a public TV station, so I don't have to pay for it.

1. Which paragraph has one main idea ?   **A   B**
2. In which paragraph are all the sentences about one idea?   **A   B**
3. Which paragraph is indented?   **A   B**
4. Which is an example of a well-written paragraph?   **A   B**

Write About It

 Write a paragraph about your favorite TV program. In the first sentence, give the name of the program. Then discuss what type of program it is, when it is on, and other information about it.

☑ **8** **Check Your Writing** You can improve your writing by having other people read and comment on it. This is called getting feedback. Work with a partner. Read and discuss your paragraphs. Revise your paragraphs if necessary. Use the checklist below to help you.

- Is there one main idea? What is it?
- Do all sentences in the paragraph develop the main idea?
- Is the paragraph indented?

GETTING STARTED

Warm Up

1 Two people watchers are at a sidewalk cafe. Who are they talking about? Listen to their conversations. Write the letter of the conversation in the corresponding box in the picture.

2 Newspapers and magazines often have articles about the private lives of movie stars, TV actors and actresses, musicians, politicians, and other famous people. Do you ever read any of them? Why or why not?

Figure It Out

Paparazzi are professional people watchers. They are photographers who take embarrassing pictures of events in the private lives of famous people. Paparazzi sell their photos to magazines and newspapers, sometimes for a lot of money.

Rock N. Roller, the famous singer and guitarist of the rock band The Broken Bones, is taking a vacation with his wife, Raquel Roller. They are staying at the Royal Hideaway Hotel so they can relax in private, away from the public eye.

Gino and Hank are paparazzi. They work for the magazine *The Rich and the Famous*. Gino and Hank want to take pictures of Rock and Raquel for their magazine.

A. **GINO:** Look, there they are!

HANK: Where?

GINO: Sitting over there by the pool. Give me the telephoto lens and some more film. Hurry! I don't want to miss anything.

HANK: What are they doing?

GINO: They're laughing and talking. They look like they're having a good time. [*click*] Wait. Rock's giving something to Raquel.

HANK: What is it?

GINO: I don't know. Wait. Raquel is opening it. Look! It's a ring. [*click*] Wow! It's huge! I'm sure it cost a fortune! [*click*] This is fantastic. Wait! Now they're getting up. I think they're going to the beach.

HANK: Let's follow them. Hurry!

B. **HANK:** What's happening now?

GINO: Rock's still lying on the towel, but Raquel isn't reading anymore. Wait! Rock's getting up. He's going into the water.

HANK: Is he swimming?

GINO: Yes, and he looks like a good swimmer. [*click*]

HANK: They say he's a health nut. He exercises twice a day at home. Plus, he plays tennis every morning and swims every afternoon after the band practices.

HANK: Wait. He's standing up now. Hey, look at Rock's hair! What's happening?

HANK: It's coming off! It's a wig! Quick! Take a picture!

C. **GINO:** I can't believe it! What a story! [*click click click*] Wait until Rock's public finds out he's bald! The magazine will pay millions for this!

HANK: Look out! The hotel security guards see us! They're running this way.

GINO: Let's get out of here!

3 Answer the questions.

   a. Why are Rock and Raquel staying at the hotel?

   b. What are Hank and Gino doing?

   c. What did Hank and Gino find out about Rock?

   d. Would you like to be famous? Why or why not?

   e. Do photographers and reporters have the right to follow famous people everywhere? Why or why not?

4 **Vocabulary Check** Complete the sentences with words or phrases from the box.

band	fortune
bald	relax
get out of	security guards
holding	towel
missed	voice
wig	nut

   a. Look! Rock has no hair! He's _____.

   b. Rock and Raquel earned millions of dollars last year. They made a _____.

   c. Gino is _____ the telephoto lens in his left hand.

   d. Rock was very tired after the band's tour. He wanted to _____ for a few days at the Royal Hideaway Hotel.

   e. There are five musicians in Rock's _____.

   f. The hotel has several _____ to keep guests safe.

   g. The police are coming. Let's _____ here before they catch us.

   h. Joe arrived late. He _____ the first part of the show.

   i. Hank loves to take pictures. He's a photography _____.

   j. Jim is over there lying on the _____.

Talk About It

An executive of the Royal Hideaway Hotel is talking to a security guard about what's happening in various parts of the hotel.

 5 With a partner, take turns being the executive and the guard. Look at the pictures. Ask and answer questions about the different places in the hotel.

Ask about present actions.

A: What's going on in the restaurant? Is anything happening there?

State present actions.

B: Well, people are eating. The waiters are serving people. Everything's fine.

GRAMMAR

The Present Progressive Tense: Present Time

To talk about habitual actions in the present, we use the simple present tense. To talk about actions that change or are happening at the present time, we use the present progressive tense.

Simple Present	Present Progressive
Rock **practices** every day.	The band **is practicing** now.

We use *still* with the present progressive to describe an action that continues in the present without changing. We use *anymore* to describe an action that stopped.

The paparazzi **are still waiting** to get a good shot of Rock.

Rock **isn't lying** on the beach **anymore**. He's swimming.

 1 You meet an old friend and you want to know what's new in his or her life. With a partner, ask and answer questions using the topics and the verbs in parentheses.

Example: Apartment (live)

A: So, are you still living in the same old apartment?

B: Yeah, I'm still living on Third Avenue.

A: And is your brother still living with you?

B: No, actually he's not living with me anymore. He moved out.

Unit 2

14

a. Job or school (work/study/teach)
b. Vacation plans (take/go)
c. Problems (have trouble/worry)
d. Free-time activities (read/paint/play)
e. Ideas of your own

The Present Progressive Tense: Future Time

We can use the present progressive to talk about planned actions in the future.
We often use future time words like *next, tomorrow, later, on Monday.*

> The Royal Hideaway Hotel **is having** a party **tonight**.
>
> Raquel and I **aren't leaving** until **next week** some time.

2 Write the correct form of the simple present or present progressive
tense on the line.

Reason

_____ **1.** The Broken Bones Band **(play)** _____ in Brazil later this week.

_____ **2.** They **(stay)** _____ at the Royal Paulista Hotel.

_____ **3.** Next week they **(perform)** _____ in Salvador de Bahia.

_____ **4.** Rock **(practice)** _____ alone for an hour every day.

_____ **5.** The band only **(play)** _____ rock music.

_____ **6.** Sticks, the drummer, **(lie)** _____ on the beach now.

_____ **7.** The band **(record)** _____ a new album next month.

_____ **8.** The band **(leave)** _____ for Salvador de Bahia after
the concert on Monday.

3 ☑ **Check Your Understanding** Now give your reason for using the
simple present or the present progressive in Exercise 2. Write **H** (habit
or routine), **N** (action happening now), or **F** (future action). Then
compare your answers with a partner's.

4 People are calling the hotel to speak to some of the hotel employees.
With a partner, take turns being the operator and the caller.

Example:

OPERATOR: Hello, Starlight Hotel.

CALLER: Hi, I'd like to speak to Ms. Aziz, the hotel manager, please.

OPERATOR: I'm sorry. She can't come to the phone right now. She's
talking to the chef. Would you like to leave a message?

CALLER: No, thanks. I'll call back later.

a. Billie Jean, the tennis instructor
b. Julia, a waitress in the restaurant
c. Paolo from the flower shop
d. Sherlock from security
e. Tomoko from the front desk
f. Marta from housekeeping
g. Angelo from the kitchen
h. Idea of your own

Stative Verbs

Generally, we do not use the present progressive with stative or non-action verbs—verbs that refer to states rather than actions. To express a continuing action with stative verbs, we usually use the simple present tense.

Common Stative Verbs	Examples
Verbs that describe mental processes: *know, remember, think, believe*	Rock **remembers** the words to all the songs.
Verbs that express feelings: *want, like, love, hate, prefer, need*	Raquel **doesn't like** the paparazzi.
Verbs that describe appearance: *be, seem, look like, appear*	Rock and Raquel **seem** happy.
Verbs that show possession: *have, own, belong*	Rock **has** seven cars.
Verbs of perception: *see, hear, taste, smell, feel, notice*	Rock and Raquel **feel** relaxed.

5 Complete the conversation with the simple present or present progressive tense. Some answers may be negative.

A: What **(1. read)** _____ you _____?

B: An article about Liz Tyler's latest marriage. It says that Liz really **(2. love)** _____ her new husband, Rudolph Valenti. They **(3. seem)** _____ so happy. Right now, in fact, they **(4. travel)** _____ around the world.

A: Everyone says her new husband **(5. be)** _____ super rich.

B: That's right. He **(6. own)** _____ homes in Paris, Rio, Zurich, and Madrid, and he **(7. build)** _____ a new house in Miami.

A: **(8. think)** _____ you _____ they will stay married?

B: I **(9. know)** _____. He's her eighth husband!

6 **Check Your Understanding** In which situations are you likely to use the present progressive tense?

- ☐ Talking about your vacation plans
- ☐ Describing a normal day at the office
- ☐ Giving your opinion about television
- ☐ Reporting the activities at a football game
- ☐ Talking about new changes in your life

Compare your answers with a partner's. Do you agree?

7 **Express Yourself** With your partner, choose one of the situations you checked above. Imagine yourselves in the situation and write a dialogue.

Listen: Where Are They?

1 **Before You Listen**

    a. What are some different places in a hotel?

    b. What do people usually do in each place? Make a list.

STRATEGY **Making Inferences** Sometimes you can guess certain information that is not directly stated because of the other words you hear. Listen for words that help you make inferences or guesses about the situation.

2 Listen to the conversations. Where are the people? Circle the place.

    a. in the clothing boutique   in the hotel lobby   on the tennis court

    b. in the bookstore   in the TV room   in the hotel lobby

    c. at the swimming pool   in the restaurant   in the gym

    d. in the snack bar   on the tennis court   at the beach

    e. in the hotel security room   in the restaurant   at the pool

3 Which words helped you figure out where the conversations were taking place? Listen to the conversations again and write the words on a sheet of paper. Compare your answers with a partner's.

Speak Out

STRATEGY **Making Appointments** When you want to meet with another person, you use certain expressions to suggest and arrange a meeting time.

Suggesting a meeting time	Can we meet at (nine o'clock)? Are you busy at (ten o'clock)?
Accepting a suggestion	That sounds good. I'll meet you in the lobby.
Suggesting another time	Sorry. I'm busy at (nine). How about (ten)? I'm busy at (ten). Are you free at (eleven)?

4 A TV executive hired a private detective to get information about another TV channel. Work with a partner. One of you is the detective and the other is the TV executive. Use the expressions above and the information in the appointment books to find a time for the meeting.

Pronunciation

> ### Syllables
> Every word has one or more beats, or syllables. For example, **needs** (needs) has one syllable, **begin** (be•gin) has two syllables, and **remembers** (re•mem•bers) has three.

5 Say the words to yourself. Predict the number of syllables for each. Then listen to the words. Write the number of syllables you hear.

a. believe _____

b. guitarist _____

c. camera _____

d. relaxes _____

e. photographer _____

f. exercises _____

g. fantastic _____

h. beaches _____

i. embarrassing _____

j. guards _____

k. actress _____

l. actresses _____

6 With your partner, take turns saying the words. Be careful to say the correct number of syllables.

READING and WRITING

Read About It

1 **Before You Read** The following article is about privacy. What do people watching and privacy have to do with each other?

The Right to Privacy

Many people enjoy learning about the rich and the famous. They spend millions of dollars yearly on newspapers and magazines that tell
5 about the private lives of rich and famous people. However, the people who enjoy reading about the private lives of others do not always like it when people watch them!

10 In the past, performers, politicians, and other people in the public eye were the only ones who worried about the right to a private life. Now, however, even ordinary people are complaining about losing their privacy. They say that they have the right to be left
15 alone and that now, because of technology, it is getting too easy to violate this right.

Today, new technology makes it possible to investigate the most private parts of people's lives. For example, some employers watch everything their employees do. They listen to personal phone calls, and they check how long their workers are at their computers. Some employers even check their employees' e-mail.

20　　Many employees know that their companies watch them at work, but they do not realize that they might be watched at home. Investigators can put secret microphones in houses or cars when no one is looking and then listen from far away. They can use tiny radios to follow drivers in their cars. And they can use video cameras to record people's actions at home—even at night when the lights are off.

25　　Computers now have records on military service, health, school grades, and work performance. People are beginning to ask why these organizations need all this information. They are also concerned because investigators can get this information without telling them. It is not surprising, then, that more and more people are worried about invasion of privacy. As a result, they are asking organizations to respect the

30　balance between the public's right to know and the individual's right to privacy.

STRATEGY **Guessing Meaning from Context** When you don't understand a word, you can often use other information in the text—the context—to figure out the meaning. Look at surrounding sentences and words to guess the meaning from context.

2 Below are five words from the reading. Use the context to figure out the meaning of each word. Choose the correct definition from the box.

> writing you keep
> equality between two things
> normal, usual
> a kind of detective
> something that others don't know
> strange, not normal

a. **ordinary** (line 13) The sentence before this one was about famous people. This sentence refers to other people who are worried about privacy, so ordinary means _____.

b. **investigators** (line 21) Investigators get information about people, so investigator means _____.

c. **secret** (line 21) This sentence refers to microphones that investigators put in people's homes or cars when no one is looking, so secret means _____.

d. **records** (line 25) This sentence is about information on health, school grades, and work performance. People keep records on computers, so records means _____.

e. **balance** (line 30) This sentence refers to two things that have the same importance, the public's right to know and the individual's right to privacy, so balance means _____.

3 Find each of the following words in the reading. Using the context, guess the meaning of each. Write the letter on the line.

_____ **1.** to complain (line 14)　　**a.** worker

_____ **2.** to violate (line 15)　　**b.** to pay attention to

_____ **3.** employee (line 17)　　**c.** to say something is wrong

_____ **4.** concerned (line 27)　　**d.** worried about

_____ **5.** to respect (line 29)　　**e.** to break

Think About It

4 Do famous people have the right to complain about an invasion of their privacy? Why or why not?

5 Is it a good idea to control employees at the workplace? (For example, phone calls, e-mail, drug and alcohol tests.) Why or why not?

Write: Narrowing a Topic

When you start with a general topic, you need to narrow it down so that you can discuss it in one paragraph. Look at the example:

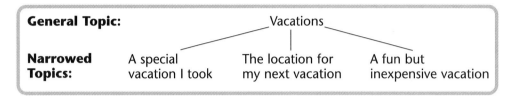

General Topic:		Vacations	
Narrowed Topics:	A special vacation I took	The location for my next vacation	A fun but inexpensive vacation

6 Here are some general writing topics. Narrow each one so that it is more suitable for one paragraph. Use your own paper.

Example:

privacy

- *the privacy teenagers need*
- *ways to protect your privacy*

a. television

b. hotels

c. music

d. sports

Write About It

7 Write a paragraph about one of your narrowed topics from the previous exercise. Remember that all the sentences in the paragraph should be about your main idea.

 8 **Check Your Writing** Read your paragraph again. Does it say what you want it to say? Use the questions in the checklist to help you. Then revise your paragraph as needed.

- Is the topic narrow enough for one paragraph?
- Is there one main idea? What is it?
- Are the verb tenses correct?

KEEPING UP WITH THE JONESES

GETTING STARTED

Warm Up

People often compare their cars, their homes, and their other possessions to what other people have. Sometimes they feel jealous. They want their things to be as good as or better than everyone else's. We say that they want to "keep up with the Joneses."

 1 Listen to each conversation. Are the people trying to "keep up with the Joneses"? Circle the answer.

   a. yes/no   **b.** yes/no   **c.** yes/no

2 What possessions are the people comparing in the conversations? What else do people compare?

Figure It Out

A.   **VAL:** Hey, look Roxy. There's a moving truck next door. I hope the new neighbors are friendly.

   ROXY: Well, I'm sure they'll be friendlier than the old ones!

   VAL: Roxy, be nice. Our old neighbors weren't as bad as you thought.

B.

VAL: I wonder if the new neighbors have any children.

ROXY: There's room for a lot of children in that house. It's much bigger than yours or mine. And the yard is huge.

VAL: Oh, Roxy, why do you always think other people's possessions are better than yours? Your yard is smaller, but a little yard is easier to take care of.

ROXY: You're right, and I still think my garden is more beautiful than theirs.

VAL: Yeah, well, it's still not as pretty as mine.

ROXY: That's only because your gardener is better than mine.

C.

ROXY: Wow! Look at the size of that TV! It's enormous! And look! They have another TV. It's even bigger than the first one!

VAL: Oh, look. Here come the new neighbors. And they have two children. The older daughter looks about the same age as your son. Isn't she pretty? Gee, she's a lot prettier than the other girls in the neighborhood.

ROXY: She's gorgeous! She's a lot richer than the other girls in the neighborhood, too! Val, don't you think she and my son will make a perfect couple?

VAL: Sure, Roxy, now I understand. If you can't keep up with the Joneses, you'll have your son marry one of them!

ROXY: That's right! If you can't beat them, marry them!

3 Answer the questions.

a. Whose house is larger, Roxy's or the new neighbors'?

b. Whose garden is prettier, Val's or Roxy's?

c. What does Roxy want her son to do? Why?

d. Why do people want to "keep up with the Joneses"?

e. Do you know anyone who tries to "keep up with the Joneses"?

f. Moving to a new house or neighborhood has advantages and disadvantages. What are they?

4 **Vocabulary Check** Complete the sentences with words from the box.

couple	neighborhood
deep	wonder
gorgeous	possessions
huge	price
jealous	size
yard	

a. I don't like living in this part of the city. I want to move to another _____.

b. The Joneses have a pool and a garden in their _____.

c. Val and Roxy _____ if the new neighbors have children.

d. Mrs Jones's daughter is really _____. I think she's the most beautiful girl in school.

e. Look at the _____ of that TV! It's enormous.

f. The Joneses' TV is larger than ours. It's _____.

g. Some people with many _____ are unhappy, but others with just a few are happy anyway.

Talk About It

 5 A real estate agent is trying to sell a house to a buyer. With a partner, take turns being the agent and the buyer. Use the information in the chart below to ask and answer questions.

Pine Street

A: I have two great houses for sale.
   Ask for a comparison.

B: Tell me about the size of the houses.
   Which one is larger, Lake Street or Pine Street?
   Make a comparison.

A: Lake Street is larger than Pine.
   It has four bedrooms.
   Ask for a comparison.

B: Which house is newer?
   Make a comparison. Ask about preference.

A: Pine Street is newer. It's only ten years old.
   Which do you like better?
   State preference.

B: I like Lake Street better because I prefer older houses.

Lake Street

	Lake Street	Pine Street	Useful Adjectives
size	4 bedrooms, 2 baths	3 bedrooms, 1 1/2 baths	big, little, large, small
age	15 years old	10 years old	new, old
price	$275,000	$300,000	expensive, inexpensive
style	traditional	modern	modern, traditional
location	near the center	far from the center	near, far

The Comparative: Talking About Differences

To talk about differences between two people, places, or things, we use the comparative form of the adjective.

One-syllable adjectives usually: *add –er*	Janet's pool is **longer than** Val's.
Two-syllable adjectives ending in *–y*: *change y to i and add –er*	Janet's garden is **prettier than** Val's.
Adjectives with two or more syllables: *use **more** or **less** … **than***	Janet's house is **more modern than** Val's. Janet's couch is **less expensive than** Val's.
Exceptions: good → better than bad → worse than far → farther than	Janet's garden is **better than** Val's.

 Look at the pictures of Nola and Atina and compare them.

Example:

A: What do you think about Nola's skirt?

B: It's shorter than Atina's and more fashionable.

a. height (tall/short)

b. appearance (pretty/attractive)

c. weight (heavy/light)

d. personality (interesting/boring/funny)

e. age (old/young)

f. clothes (expensive/cheap/fashionable)

g. hair (long/short/curly/straight)

Atina   **Nola**

 Compare the following items. Use an adjective that fits the category.

Example:

(size) Luxemburg/Lithuania
Luxemburg is a smaller country than Lithuania.

a.	(size)	Mexico City/Cairo
b.	(price)	apartment in New York/apartment in Tokyo
c.	(age)	Buenos Aires/Madrid
d.	(appearance)	modern furniture/antique furniture
e.	(distance)	Mars/Jupiter
f.	(height)	Mt. Fuji/Mt. Everest
g.	(quality)	German cars/American cars
h.	(length)	The Amazon River/The Nile River

Talking About Differences: *not as ... as*

We also use *not as ... as* to talk about the difference between two items. This form is common because it is less critical.

Less critical		More critical
Roxy's kitchen is**n't as clean as** Val's.	=	Val's kitchen is **dirtier than** Roxy's.
It is**n't as modern as** Val's either.	=	Val's kitchen is **less modern than** Roxy's.

 Rewrite the sentences to be less critical.

Example: Roxy's house is smaller than Val's.
> *Val's house isn't as large as Roxy's.*

  a. Val's garden is less beautiful than Roxy's.
  b. Janet's couch is less comfortable than Roxy's.
  c. Janet's car is slower than Roxy's.
  d. Val's daughter is less attractive than Roxy's.
  e. Roxy is less polite than Janet.

Talking About Similarities

We use *as* + adjective + *as* and *the same* (+ noun +) *as* to show that two items are the same. To show that two items are almost the same, we use *like* and *similar to*.

Roxy's car is **as old as** Val's.	=	Roxy's car is **the same age as** Val's.
Roxy's furniture is **like** Val's.	=	Roxy's furniture is **similar to** Val's.

 Read about Franny and Pia and make a list of their similarities.

  Franny and Pia are good friends. They were both born in 1985. Both are 5 feet 7 inches tall. They each weigh 120 pounds. Both girls have brown eyes and dark hair. Each gets excellent grades at school. Both girls are active in school events and very popular. They are both wealthy and generous. Too bad they don't exist!

Example:

Franny is the same age as Pia.

  Check Your Understanding Check the situations in which you are likely to use comparatives. Compare your answers with a partner's.

☐ Giving directions to a stranger
☐ Deciding which computer to buy
☐ Choosing between two people for a job
☐ Deciding on a vacation spot
☐ Talking about your preference in music

6 **Express Yourself** Work with a partner. Choose one of the situations from Exercise 5, and write a dialogue using comparative forms.

Example:

A: So, who do you think is the better candidate for the job?

B: Well, Tony's more experienced, but he doesn't seem as bright as Sandra.

A: I think Sandra's a lot friendlier, and she'll get along better with her colleagues.

B: So, do we agree on Sandra?

Now practice the dialogue with your partner.

LISTENING and SPEAKING

Listen: Choosing a Restaurant

1 **Before You Listen** What do you consider when you buy or rent a house or apartment? Number your answers from 1 (most important) to 8 (least important). Compare your choices with those of a partner.

_____ price _____ number of rooms _____ yard _____ age

_____ size _____ location _____ garden _____ view

 Listening for Criteria When comparing items, it is normal to use criteria or standards. Listening for the criteria will help you understand the comparison.

2 Listen to the conversation. A woman is trying to pick out a restaurant. Look at the criteria in the box. Circle the ones she uses.

age	price
size	food
cleanliness	noise
popularity	service

3 Listen to the conversation again. Check the correct column.

Criteria	Andy's Restaurant	Starlight Diner
cheaper	☐	☐
newer	☐	☐
noisier	☐	☐
cleaner	☐	☐
smaller	☐	☐
better food	☐	☐
more crowded	☐	☐

Pronunciation

Syllable Stress

In words of two or more syllables, one syllable is longer, louder, and higher. This is the stressed syllable. Listen to the words. The stressed syllable is in bold type.

com**pare**   **jeal**ous   pos**se**ssions   **neigh**bor

  4 Listen to the words. Underline the stressed syllable in each word.

a. entertain   d. understand   g. disagree

b. garage   e. noisier   h. expensive

c. customer   f. attractive   i. enormous

5 Work with a partner. Take turns saying the words aloud, focusing on correct syllable stress.

Speak Out

 Agreeing and Disagreeing In conversation, it's customary to ask if others agree with you. It's also common to explain why you agree or disagree with someone.

Asking for Agreement	Agreeing	Disagreeing
Do you agree?	I think so too, because …	I'm sorry, but I don't agree with you because …
Do you feel the same way?	Yes, I know how you feel.	No, I don't feel that way because …
What do you think?	I don't think so either.	I'm sorry, but I think …

6 In small groups, discuss which of the two alternatives you like better. Give reasons.

Example:

Tom: I think city life is better than country life.

Ann: So do I. There is so much more to do. What do you think?

Bob: I agree with Tom.

Sue: Well, I don't agree. I like the country better because you don't have to face crowds.

Ed: I disagree. Farm life is hard work.

a. country life/city life

b. car/motorcycle

c. private/public school

d. living with your family/living alone

e. vacation in summer/vacation in winter

Unit 3

Read About It

1 Before You Read

   a. We all have certain ideas about different groups of people such as movie stars, people from other countries, or politicians. We call these ideas stereotypes. What other groups of people do we stereotype? Make a list.

   b. Work in a small group. Give examples of stereotypes. Do you think that most stereotypes are true? Explain your answer. Why do people form stereotypes? How can we break them?

STRATEGY **Identifying Main Ideas** As you read, you should always try to identify the main ideas. Each paragraph has its own main idea, often stated in the first sentence in the paragraph. The other sentences give more information about the main idea.

MALLcrawlers
A Teenage Stereotype

Many people believe that American teenagers think only about buying goods. They say teens today want all the fashionable clothes, shoes, music, and sports equipment that their
5 friends have, all the things that they see advertised on TV and in magazines. When American teens get money, the critics say, they walk around the shopping mall for hours at a time. Teens who pass the time this way are called "mall crawlers." Is this
10 stereotype of American teenagers true?

     It is true that more American teens have money to spend and that they are spending it at the mall. Research companies tell us, for example, that 12- to 19-year-olds spent over $109 billion in
15 1995, a 38% increase over 1990. Those numbers are even bigger today because almost 50% of teens 16 and older have part-time jobs after school or on weekends. In addition, experts predict that the teenage population will be larger
20 than ever before, reaching almost 35 million by the year 2010. This means that teenage consumers will play an even more important economic role in the future of the United States.

     American teens are wealthier and work harder than before, but not all 25 of their interests center on clothes, music, and movies at the mall. Around 30% of working teens save money in order to go to college. Others help in the purchase of a family computer or contribute to the family grocery budget. In 30 addition, many American teens give their time to volunteer work and community service. And of course at school, competition for good grades to get into college is as tough as ever. With so many important responsibilities, it is unlikely that 35 American teens spend all their time and money crawling the mall. It is easy but unfair to stereotype them in such a way. ∎

2 What is the main idea of each paragraph of the reading? In which sentence does the main idea occur? Check your answers with a partner.

3 Use the context to match the words from the reading with their meanings.

_____ **1.** fashionable (line 3)　　　**a.** rise in number

_____ **2.** mall crawlers (line 9)　　**b.** to give money or help

_____ **3.** increase (line 15)　　　　**c.** people who buy goods

_____ **4.** population (line 19)　　　**d.** buying

_____ **5.** consumers (line 21)　　　**e.** popular at the moment

_____ **6.** purchase (line 29)　　　　**f.** people who walk around a mall

_____ **7.** to contribute (line 30)　　**g.** money set aside

_____ **8.** budget (line 30)　　　　　**h.** number of people

Think About It

4 What are some other stereotypes about teenagers? Are they true or false? Explain your answers.

5 Do teenagers have the right to spend all the money they earn on themselves? Why or why not?

Write: The Topic Sentence

The main idea of a paragraph is usually introduced in the first sentence. This is called the topic sentence. The topic sentence is the most important sentence in the paragraph. It focuses the topic by giving the writer's main idea, opinion, or feeling about the subject.

A good topic sentence is not too general or too narrow. Imagine you want to write about your neighbor's new car. Look at three possible topic sentences and the comments about each:

　a. My neighbor has many possessions.
　　Too general. This sentence is not focused on the new car.

　b. My neighbor's new car is metallic blue.
　　Too narrow. This sentence is about only one aspect of the car.

　c. My neighbor's new car is fantastic.
　　Just right. This paragraph can explain why the car is fantastic.

6 Decide if the topic sentences below are too general, too narrow, or just right. Discuss your answers with the class.

   a. Houses are expensive.

   b. My TV cost $450.00.

   c. My new TV has several amazing features.

   d. My roommate sometimes annoys me.

   e. There are four important criteria in choosing a house.

   f. The topic of this paper is television.

Write About it

7 Write a paragraph about one of your favorite possessions. Explain why the possession is important to you. Look at the model.

> Over the years I have collected many items, but my most valuable possession is a ring my husband gave me. He gave it to me a few months before we were married. He spent a long time looking for the right ring, and he was very proud of his choice. The ring is a sapphire set on a simple gold band. The sapphire is deep blue and is surrounded by two small diamonds. The ring is beautiful and was probably expensive, but I treasure it because it reminds me of my husband. Every time I wear it, I am closer to him.

8 Exchange papers with a partner. Give feedback to your partner to help him or her make the paragraph as clear as possible.

9 **Check Your Writing** Use your partner's comments and the questions below to revise your paragraph.

- Is the paragraph indented?
- Does the paragraph have a topic sentence? Where is it? Does it state the main idea of the paragraph?
- Is the topic sentence neither too general nor too narrow?

1 Complete the passage with the correct form of the verbs in the box. Use the simple present or present progressive tense.

learn	watch
think	love
enjoy	know
spend	

Many parents think that their children **(1.)** _____ too much time in front of the TV, but TV can be educational. For example, Sylvia and Eddie **(2.)** _____ an interesting TV program on animals now. Another program they **(3.)** _____ is about the latest developments in computer technology. Sylvia now **(4.)** _____ how to send e-mail and how to use the Internet. Eddie **(5.)** _____ about all the new computer games. Sylvia and Eddie's parents don't worry about TV; they **(6.)** _____ their children **(7.)** _____ a lot from the programs they **(8.)** _____.

2 Complete the conversation with the correct form of the verbs in parentheses. Use the simple present or present progressive tense.

Bob: Hey, Pat. What **(1. do)** _____ you _____?

Pat: Hi, Bob. I **(2. listen)** _____ to the latest CD by The Broken Bones Band.

Bob: Oh yeah? I **(3. hear)** _____ they have some great songs on there.

Pat: They do. I really **(4. like)** _____ "Crash" and "Forget About It."

Bob: I **(5. know,** *neg.***)** _____ those songs, but I love their old ones.

Pat: What **(6. do)** _____ you _____ after class?
(7. want) _____ you _____ to come over to my place and listen to their new CD?

Bob: That **(8. sound)** _____ great, but I can't. I **(9. have)** _____ an appointment. I **(10. meet)** _____ an old friend this evening.

Pat: Too bad. Another time, maybe.

3 Complete the sentences with the appropriate time expression from the box.

right now	every year
this year	tonight
once a day	once in a while
always	rarely

a. The Broken Bones Band works hard and records a new album _____.

b. David _____ watches TV on weekends; he likes to be outdoors.

c. We are going to the movies _____ after dinner.

d. My favorite news program is coming on _____.

e. If you are a couch potato, you should try turning off the TV _____.

f. The boss is not happy because Mary is _____ late for work.

4 Complete the paragraph with the comparative form of the adjectives in parentheses.

Mark's computer is **(1. new)** _____ than Zack's. It also has a **(2. powerful)** _____ processor and a much **(3. large)** _____ memory. Mark's computer is **(4. fast)** _____ than Zack's, too. However, Zack's computer is **(5. easy)** _____ to use. Zack's is also **(6. small)** _____ and **(7. attractive)** _____ in design. I think Zack's computer is **(8. good)** _____ than Mark's, but I wonder which one was **(9. expensive)** _____.

5 Rewrite the comparative sentences so that the meaning is the same.

a. Marty's house is dirtier than Teddy's.   _Marty's house isn't as clean as Teddy's._

b. Lou's new bike is cheaper than Jan's.   _____

c. _____   Mark's garden isn't as pretty as Tim's.

d. Pauline is less intelligent than Eve.   _____

e. _____   Susan's writing isn't as good as Mia's.

f. Bob is poorer than Sam.   _____

Vocabulary Review

Use the words in the box to complete the sentences.

commercial	enormous
crowded	relax
bored	follow
embarrassing	miss
jealous	security
possession	wonder

1. Look! There's Rock! Let's _____ him and try to take his picture!

2. I'm _____. Can't you find a more interesting program to watch?

3. Rock and Raquel Roller went to a luxury hotel to get away from fans and _____.

4. That is the biggest swimming pool in this neighborhood. It's _____!

5. I think Roxy is _____ of Val's prize-winning garden.

6. Let's go somewhere else to eat. It's too _____ here.

7. Rock! Call _____! Someone is taking photos of us through the window!

8. Our program will continue right after this _____. Stay tuned!

9. I _____ if Rock N. Roller wears a wig. I'd love to find out.

10. I never _____ my favorite TV shows.

AND THE BEAT GOES ON!

Ricky Martin

Madonna

Placido Domingo

Elvis Presley

Celine Dion

Will Smith

GETTING STARTED

Warm Up

1 People in all cultures enjoy music. What kinds of music are popular in your country? What kinds do you like?

2 You are going to listen to different selections of music. What kind of music is each one? Write the number of the selection on the line.

____ classical   ____ jazz

____ opera   ____ rap

____ folk   ____ soul

____ country and western   ____ rock and roll

Figure It Out

3 Look at the singers above. What do you know about them? Think about:

- biographical information
- albums and songs
- personal life

4 Which singer is each article about?

A. _____

He was born in the United States in the city of Philadelphia. When he was only twelve, he showed great talent as a rapper.
5 With Jazzy Jeff, his childhood friend and partner, he made two albums which sold thousands of copies and won important music awards. In fact, because of his rap music hits, he
10 was already a millionaire at eighteen! In 1990, he surprised his fans and became the star of a popular TV comedy series, which lasted until 1996. Then he decided
15 to perform in movies. He acted in a film almost every year from 1993 to 1998. He became even more popular after he made an adventure movie in which he wore a black suit
20 and black sunglasses and saved the world.

B. _____

One of fourteen brothers and sisters, she spent her childhood in Charlemagne, a town in Quebec, Canada. At age five, she already showed talent as a songwriter and
25 singer in French. She recorded a "demo" (demonstration album) when she was only twelve, and two years later became a performing star in Quebec. Well known in Canada and France, she participated in the Eurovision Song Contest in 1988, and won. As a result, people in
30 Europe, Russia, Australia, and the Middle East bought her albums. She longed to be popular in the United States and England too, and so she worked very hard to learn English. Her songs in English became instant hits, and she won many awards for her albums and for songs on movie
35 soundtracks such as *Titanic*.

C. _____

He was born in Spain in 1941, but moved to Mexico with his family when he was eight years old. As a child, he did not know
40 whether he wanted to be a soccer player or an orchestra conductor when he grew up. Both his parents were well-known singers. He made his first appearance in a musical comedy, but later became an
45 opera singer. He performed in operas all over the world. His dream of becoming a conductor came true, too—he made his first appearance as a conductor in
50 London. He also recorded albums of popular songs, which made him even more famous.

 5 **Vocabulary Check** Use the context to match the words with the correct meaning.

_____ **1.** talent (line 4)   **a.** to change from child to adult
_____ **2.** awards (line 8)   **b.** ability to do something well
_____ **3.** hits (line 9)   **c.** famous
_____ **4.** to perform (line 15)   **d.** to want very much
_____ **5.** to participate in (line 28) **e.** prizes
_____ **6.** to long (line 31)   **f.** songs or shows that are successful
_____ **7.** instant (line 33)   **g.** immediate
_____ **8.** conductor (line 41)   **h.** to enter
_____ **9.** to grow up (line 42)   **i.** to act, sing, or dance for the public
_____ **10.** well-known (line 43)   **j.** person who directs an orchestra

Talk About It

 6 A reporter from a music magazine is interviewing Rock N. Roller. Look at the start of their interview. With a partner, take turns being the reporter and Rock. Use the cues to continue the interview.

Ask about past action.

A: So, Rock, when did you decide to become a rock singer?

Tell about past action.

B: When I was twelve or thirteen. At first I wanted to be a doctor. Then I changed my mind.

Question	**Answer**
a. reason for becoming a rock singer	love of rock music
b. date of first performance	July 15, 1996
c. place of first performance	the Rock Land Club, New York City
d. date of first CD	January 21, 1998
e. people important to your music	my first guitar teacher, Mr. Segovia
f. training and musical education	four years at Jillian School of Music

GRAMMAR

The Simple Past Tense: Past Events

We use the simple past tense to talk about actions completed in the past. For regular verbs, add *–ed* or *–d* to the base verb. For irregular verbs, see pages 129–130.

A: The band U2 **performed** at Tower Theater last night. Everyone **loved** the concert. It **turned out** great.

B: **Did** they **sing** their latest hit?

A: Of course. But they **didn't play** my favorite song, "Indigo."

B: Maybe they only **wanted** to do their new songs.

A: Yeah probably. Anyway, we **had** a fantastic time.

1 Read the passage and underline the past tense verbs.

Oum Kalsoum

Oum Kalsoum was one of the most famous Arab singers of the twentieth century. She grew up in a village in Egypt. Her father sang religious songs at weddings and other events. When he noticed his daughter's voice, he gave her lessons and included her in his performances. She didn't go to the university, but she soon became very successful.

Oum Kalsoum was popular because she had a powerful voice. When she performed, people really listened. She recorded 300 songs and made six movies. Even today you can hear her music all over the Middle East.

2 Now put the verbs that you underlined in Exercise 1 in the correct category.

Regular Verbs   Irregular Verbs

_____   _____

_____   _____

3 Work with a partner. Use the cues to make questions about Oum Kalsoum. Then use the information from Exercise 1 to answer them.

Example: Who/Oum Kalsoum

A: Who was Oum Kalsoum?

B: She was one of the most famous Arab singers of the twentieth century.

a. Where/grow up   d. Why/popular

b. What/father/do   e. How many songs/record

c. go/university

4 Complete the passage with the correct form of the verb. Some answers may be negative.

John Lennon **(1. be)** _____
born in 1940 in Liverpool, England, where
he **(2. grow up)** _____. As a
teenager, he **(3. meet)** _____ Paul
McCartney, and they **(4. begin)** _____
to write songs together. After several years, they
(5. form) _____ a new group called
The Beatles with George Harrison and Pete Best.
However, Best **(6. stay)** _____ in the
group. Ringo Starr **(7. join)** _____
the group in place of Best. In 1964, the group
(8. perform) _____ its first hit song,
"Love Me Do." Between the years 1962 and 1968,
The Beatles **(9. be)** _____ the most
famous group in the world.

In 1970, The Beatles **(10. break up)** _____, and
Lennon **(11. decide)** _____ to perform alone. Between
1969 and 1972, he and his wife, Yoko Ono, **(12. do)** _____
a series of charity concerts together. In 1975, John and Yoko
(13. have) _____ a son. John
(14. leave) _____ his music
career to raise their child. Five years
later, he **(15. go)** _____ back to
his music. Tragically, in 1983, Lennon
was shot in New York. Lennon's life
(16. end) _____, but his
music lives on today.

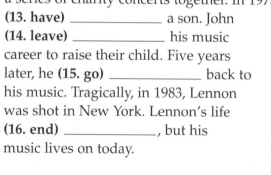

5 Work with a partner. Use the information in the chart to take turns asking and answering questions.

Example:

A: Who composed the opera *Carmen*?

B: Georges Bizet did.

Who	Did	What?
a. Georges Bizet		the opera *Aida*
b. Giuseppe Verdi	paint	the piano
c. Pablo Picasso	write	electricity
d. Shah Jahan	build	the play *Hamlet*
e. Paul McCartney	compose	the painting *Guernica*
f. Miguel de Cervantes	invent	the Taj Mahal
g. Benjamin Franklin	discover	the novel *Don Quixote*
h. Bartolomeo Cristofori		the opera *Carmen*
i. William Shakespeare		the song "Yesterday"

6 **Check Your Understanding** In which situations are you likely to use the past tense? Check your answers with a partner's.

☐ Talking about your next vacation

☐ Telling a story

☐ Describing your first concert

☐ Explaining how to make coffee

☐ Talking about the life of Mozart

Adverbs of Sequence with the Simple Past Tense

> To tell the order of events, we can use adverbs of sequence, such as *first, later, next, then, after that, soon,* and *finally.*

7 Read the paragraph and underline all the adverbs of sequence.

Rosemary Brown

Although Franz Liszt, the famous composer, died in 1886, a woman in England, Rosemary Brown, says she first saw his spirit when she was seven. Many years later, in 1964, she says Liszt returned and gave her compositions he wrote after his death. Some time later, he introduced her to the spirits of Bach, Beethoven, Chopin, Mozart, and other composers. Soon afterward, they too asked her to write down the music they composed after their deaths. With only two years of musical training, Rosemary wrote down more than 500 pieces of music. Many experts believed the dead composers had actually written the compositions. Finally, Rosemary recorded the album of spirit compositions in 1971.

8 Can you replace the adverbs of sequence in the paragraph from Exercise 7 with any of these? If so, where?

    a. then   **d.** after that

    b. in the end   **e.** next

    c. before then

 9 **Express Yourself** Pick one of your favorite musicians or artists. Prepare a short biographical sketch of the artist. Use the passages in this unit as models. Take notes to organize your ideas.

Then, in a small group, present your artist. Be sure to use the past tense and adverbs of sequence to show the order of events. Be prepared to answer questions from members of your group.

LISTENING and SPEAKING

Listen: Music Around the World

1 **Before You Listen**

    a. People use music in many different ways. For example, people use music to put babies to sleep. List as many uses of music as you can.

    b. Why do you listen to music?

 Listening to Complete a Chart When you listen and take notes, you sometimes have to complete a chart. Charts help organize information. Before listening, look at the chart carefully to see what to listen for.

Wooden drums

Steel drums

Camels in the desert

You are going to listen to part of a talk about different kinds of music. Look at the chart to see what information you will have to fill in. Then, listen carefully and fill in the chart.

Type of Music	Place of Origin	Use
1. wooden drums		to communicate
2. steel drums	Barbados, West Indies	
3. koto music		to accompany plays
4. Vedic song	India	
5. Huda song		to stop spirits

Pronunciation

The –ed Ending

We pronounce the past tense ending of regular verbs in three ways, depending on the final sound of the verb.

/t/ after voiceless sounds: tal**ked,** hel**ped,** wis**hed**

/d/ after voiced sounds: perfor**med,** liv**ed,** liste**ned**

/ɪd/ after **–d** and **–t** endings: wan**ted,** recor**ded,** visi**ted**

  Listen to the dialogue, focusing on the underlined past tense endings. For each ending, decide if you hear **/t/, /d/,** or **/ɪd/**. Then practice saying the dialogue.

A: So you visi<u>ted</u> the exhibit on African-American music I recommend<u>ed</u>?

B: Yes, and you were right. I lov<u>ed</u> it. I rent<u>ed</u> the Tour on Tape just as you suggest<u>ed</u>.

A: So, tell me what you learn<u>ed</u>.

B: I discover<u>ed</u> that rap start<u>ed</u> out in the streets of New York City in the 1970s. Performers us<u>ed</u> bits of funk and hard rock and other sounds as background to their lyrics.

A: Yeah, I know. I visi<u>ted</u> the exhibit three times.

Speak Out

 Keeping a Conversation Going You can keep a conversation going by asking questions and by showing interest.

What happened after that?

How interesting!

Then what?

Oh, no!

Oh, really?

That's amazing.

4 Work with a partner. Think of one of your first-time experiences, such as your first concert or your first airplane flight. What happened? How did you feel? Take turns talking about your experiences. Use the expressions in the box to keep your conversation going.

Read About It

1 **Before You Read** In a small group, brainstorm the topic of jazz. Make a list of everything that comes to your mind when you hear the word "jazz." Share your ideas with the class.

STRATEGY **Noticing Chronological Order** When you read, it is important to understand the order in which events happen in time. Pay attention to signals such as dates, and adverbs of time, such as *then, next, after that,* and *later.*

The Story of Jazz

The word "jazz" has just four letters, but it covers a multitude of sounds. No definition completely describes it. In the approximately 100 years of its history, jazz has gone through many changes in style—from the earliest blues, to
5 Dixieland, to the Charleston, to swing, to boogie-woogie, to mambo. Jazz musicians of all these different styles do two things in common: they all make sudden, surprising changes in rhythm, and they all improvise (freely compose and invent music as they play, spontaneously). In other words, jazz
10 singers and musicians follow their own inspiration, but they come together to speak the same musical language.

The musical language of jazz began in New Orleans, Louisiana, and came from the mixture of cultures there at that time—old French, new American, Black, and Indian. People
15 used music to accompany daily life, and gradually this music took on all the feelings and emotions of daily life, such as happiness, sadness, anger, and resignation. The more emotion players put into jazz, the more popular it became.

Soon, jazz spread from New Orleans to Memphis and,
20 after that, to Chicago. In Chicago, the music changed to reflect the 1920s, a time of illegal alcohol and gangsters like Al Capone. At this time, jazz was not considered very respectable. Jazz became more respectable in the 1930s as "big bands" filled dance halls and ballrooms with thousands
25 of people, and fans supported their favorite bands just as they did their favorite baseball teams. In the 1940s and 1950s, individual musicians such as Charlie Parker and Duke Ellington received more attention than the bands, and the popularity of jazz continued to grow.
30 Today jazz lives on. We hear it in musical comedies, movies, TV programs, and TV commercials. Jazz musicians of today still experiment with new forms, and performers such as Gato Barbieri, Wynton Marsalis, and Geri Allen continue to delight their fans with creative and exciting music.

Preservation Hall, New Orleans

Preservation Hall Jazz Band

Louis Armstrong

2 Answer the questions.

   a. Why is it difficult to define jazz?

   b. Why wasn't jazz very respectable in the 1920s?

   c. When were big bands popular?

3 Put the events in the correct order. Write 1 (first) to 6 (last).

   _____ Individual musicians got more attention than big bands.

   _____ Jazz spread from New Orleans to Memphis to Chicago.

   _____ Jazz became more respectable as the big bands filled dance halls.

   _____ Jazz started in New Orleans almost 100 years ago.

   _____ In the 1920s, jazz reflected the times of illegal alcohol and Al Capone.

   _____ Jazz performers continue to delight audiences.

4 Use the context to guess the meanings of the words. Circle the letter.

1. a multitude of (lines 1–2)
  a. few
  b. many
  c. composition

2. history (line 3)
  a. past
  b. present
  c. future

3. blues (line 4)
  a. a jazz style
  b. a color
  c. a jazz singer

4. spontaneously (line 9)
  a. very quickly
  b. with singing
  c. without planning

5. to accompany (line 15)
  a. to change
  b. to go together with
  c. to improve

6. spread (line 19)
  a. traveled
  b. went away
  c. changed

Think About It

5 Why do you think music exists in every culture of the world?

6 Is your country well known for a certain type of music? Explain.

Write: Supporting Sentences

The topic sentence of a paragraph is followed by a number of other sentences called supporting sentences. These sentences make up the body of a paragraph. In a well-written paragraph, all of the supporting sentences give more information about the topic sentence.

7 Read the paragraph and answer the questions below.

   a. What is the topic sentence?

   b. How many supporting sentences are there?

   c. What information do the supporting sentences give about the topic sentence?

> In our city, there are several places where you can listen to music in the summer. At least twice a month, the City Orchestra performs in the Miller Outdoor Theater in Hermann Park. These concerts are especially popular because they are free. In Tranquility Park, rock groups sometimes come and give open-air concerts. Finally, on Saturday and Sunday evenings, jazz musicians perform in the downtown Pavilion. The summer is a great time for music lovers in our city.

8 Read the following paragraphs. In each paragraph, find the one sentence that does not support the topic sentence. Cross it out.

A.

*G*IUSEPPE VERDI, a well-loved composer of opera, had a very simple musical beginning. His first musical lessons came from a priest in his church. He also liked to read. When he was ten years old, he moved to the small city of Busseto to play music for the church there. Two years later, he became the main church organist. In four years, Verdi became the best organist of the area.

Verdi's opera *Aida*

B.

Verdi's music is full of emotion. The stories of his operas are full of love, death, romance, and excitement. He used his music to show these feelings. He didn't like the music of Richard Wagner, another opera composer. He worked hard on melody, the main part of a song, because he thought that melody was a very important way to show emotion.

Write About It

9 Write a paragraph about your favorite composer, singer, or musical group. First, brainstorm everything you know about the artist. Focus on one central idea. Write a topic sentence and develop it with supporting sentences.

10 Exchange papers with a partner. Ask questions about parts where you want more information.

11 **Check Your Writing** Make revisions based on your partner's comments and the questions below.

- Does the paragraph have a topic sentence? Is there one main idea?
- Do all the supporting sentences give information about the topic sentence?
- Is the sequence of events clearly marked with adverbs of sequence or dates?

GETTING STARTED

Warm Up

🎧 **1** If you escape a dangerous situation, we say you had a "close call." Listen to the conversations and look at the pictures. Write the letter of the conversation in the box. There is one extra picture.

2 What do people do in these emergencies?

Figure It Out

Read the following news report to find out people's reactions to a close call with a tornado.

And now …
today's weather. A tornado
struck Park City Airport at 11:15 this
morning. It damaged the airport
building and destroyed a plane.
Several people were hurt. Let's go
to Al Stevens at the airport …

Unit 5

43

A.   **AL STEVENS:**   For the people at Park City Airport, this morning's tornado was a real close call. Let's get these people's reactions. [*to airport official*] Excuse me, Ma'am. What was happening here at the airport when the storm struck?

AIRPORT OFFICIAL: Well, everything was going fine. Planes were taking off and landing on time. Passengers were waiting at the gate to get on Flight 62. Then, suddenly, we saw a black cloud coming closer and closer!

AL STEVENS: What happened then?

AIRPORT OFFICIAL: The tornado hit the plane and destroyed it. There was baggage and broken glass all over. I thought it was the end! I was really afraid.

AL STEVENS: Well, that's not surprising. Thank you, Ma'am.

B.   **AL STEVENS:**   Excuse me, Sir. Could you tell me about this morning's tornado?

TICKET AGENT: Well, I was having a problem with an awful person. While passengers were checking in, this man tried to get ahead of a woman and her children. She got angry and told him to wait his turn, and he started to shout at her. They were having a terrible argument.

AL STEVENS: Then what happened?

TICKET AGENT: Well, all of a sudden, the storm hit and the windows shattered. Glass was all over the floor. People were screaming and running away from the windows. Babies were crying and alarms were ringing. Naturally, I hid behind the counter.

C. **AL STEVENS:** What about you? What were you doing when the storm struck?

TEENAGER: Well, my friend Jeff and I were getting some lunch at the snack bar. As he was taking his food back to the table, the lights went out, and he fell into the salad bar. At first I was afraid, but later I thought it was funny when I saw he had lettuce in his hair!

AL STEVENS: Thank you. [*to camera*] And those are some of the reactions to this morning's tornado. This is Al Stevens at the Park City Airport.

3 Answer the questions.
   a. When did the tornado strike?
   b. What was happening when the tornado struck?
   c. What happened to Jeff?
   d. Are there dangerous weather conditions in your country? What are they? How often do they occur?

4 **Vocabulary Check** Read the sentences. From the words in the box, find a synonym for the underlined word or words below and write it on the line.

argument	hid
get ahead of	passengers
shouting	landing
caused	taking off
damaged	struck
close call	checking in

_____ **a.** People were <u>giving their tickets and suitcases to the agent</u>.

_____ **b.** We had a <u>dangerous experience</u>, but we didn't get hurt.

_____ **c.** Planes were <u>leaving</u> on time.

_____ **d.** Planes were <u>arriving</u> on time.

_____ **e.** The <u>people who are traveling on the plane</u> are waiting in line.

_____ **f.** A man tried to <u>move in front of</u> a woman.

_____ **g.** The tornado <u>hit</u> at 11:15.

_____ **h.** The tornado <u>created</u> a lot of damage.

_____ **i.** Two customers were having an <u>angry conversation</u>.

_____ **j.** A man and a woman were <u>speaking loudly</u> at each other.

_____ **k.** A ticket agent <u>got</u> behind the counter so that no one could see him.

Talk About It

A reporter is interviewing more people at the airport.

Ask about continuing actions in the past.

A: What were you doing when the storm hit?

Tell about continuing actions in the past.

B: I was waiting to check in.

---

5 With a partner, take turns being the reporter and one of the interviewees.

a. a cook in the snack bar

b. a clerk at the magazine stand

c. a pilot in a plane

d. a passenger at the gate

e. a passenger at the baggage claim

f. a taxi driver at the taxi stand

GRAMMAR

The Simple Past and the Past Progressive Tenses

To talk about a finished action in the past, we use the simple past tense. We use the past progressive tense (*was/were* + verb–*ing*) to show a continuing action or an incomplete action in the past interrupted by another action.

Simple Past	Yesterday, a tornado **struck** the airport. (*finished*)
Past Progressive	A baby **was crying** at the airport. (*continuing*)
	Passengers **were checking in** when the storm hit. (*interrupted*)

1 Read the sentences and circle the appropriate verb form.

When the storm hit, ...

_____	**a.** an agent	**was checking in/checked in**	passengers.
_____	**b.** passengers	**were standing/stood**	in line.
_____	**c.** the airport official	**was seeing/saw**	the black cloud.
_____	**d.** the lights	**were going/went**	out.
_____	**e.** the windows	**were shattering/shattered.**	
_____	**f.** people	**were screaming/screamed.**	
_____	**g.** alarms	**were ringing/rang.**	

2 In Exercise 1, which of the actions finished quickly and which were continuing? Write **F** for finished and **C** for continuing on the lines.

Time Clauses with *When, While, As*

When, while, and *as* introduce time clauses that show that two actions happened at the same time. *While* and *as* usually introduce a continuing action; *when* introduces a finished or completed action.

> **While** we were checking in, the tornado struck.
>
> **As** the plane was landing, a tornado hit.
>
> **When** the storm came in, I was driving to the airport.

Time clauses can come before or after the main clause, but the punctuation changes.

> **When the storm hit**, I was driving to the airport.
>
> I was driving to the airport **when the storm hit**.

3 Complete the passage with the correct form of the verb.

Poon Lim, a Chinese sailor, had a close call in 1943. He
(1. work) _____ on a British ship when a torpedo
(2. hit) _____ it. Poon Lim **(3. jump)** _____ into
the water. The ship **(4. explode)** _____ while he
(5. swim) _____ away from it.

Poon Lim was afraid. Then as he **(6. try)** _____
to keep his head above water, he **(7. see)** _____ a
raft. The raft **(8. save)** _____ his life!

Poon Lim got into the raft. There was food inside. While he
(9. wait) _____ for help, he **(10. eat)** _____ the
food and **(11. drink)** _____ rainwater. When the food
was gone, he **(12. start)** _____ to fish.

Poon Lim was on the raft for 133 days. Then, some Brazilian
fishermen **(13. find)** _____ him on August 3, 1943.
While he **(14. recover)** _____ from his close call, the
United States **(15. invite)** _____ him to live in the U.S.A.

4 Yesterday afternoon at 12:30, a helicopter hit the side of
a tall building. Describe what people were doing when
the accident happened. With a partner, ask and answer
questions using the cues below.

Example: (Mary/hear/sirens) (shop at mall)

A: What was Mary doing when she heard the sirens?

B: She was shopping at the mall when she heard the sirens.

a. (Gloria/hear/noise)	(wait/traffic light)
b. (Bonnie/smell/smoke)	(buy/newspaper)
c. (Tim/feel/explosion)	(work/desk)
d. (Neal/see/accident)	(cross/street)
e. (Liz/hear/explosion)	(get/coffee)
f. (Mike/feel/explosion)	(talk/his boss)
g. (Marco/see/fire)	(eat/lunch)
h. (Sue/hear/crash)	(wait/bus)

☑ 5 Check Your Understanding In which situations are you likely to use the simple past and the past progressive tense? Check your answers with the class.

☐ Talking about a close call

☐ Talking about a strange event on the bus

☐ Describing an earthquake experience

☐ Describing your recent trip to Bangkok

☐ Explaining why you were late

☐ Comparing a hurricane to a tornado

6 Express Yourself Work with a partner. Choose one of the situations you checked above. Imagine yourselves in the situation and write a dialogue.

LISTENING and SPEAKING

Listen: A News Story

1 Before You Listen How often do you listen to the news? What is your favorite part of the news—the local news, the international news, human interest stories, the sports, or the weather?

STRATEGY **Listening for Sequence** To understand the sequence of events in a story, listen for time words such as *first, then, after, finally, when, while,* and *as.*

2 Listen to the news story. Put the events in the correct order by numbering them from 1 to 7.

_____ **a.** Ms. Martin pushed the man while he was trying to run away.

_____ **b.** Ms. Martin hit the man with a bottle of milk.

_1_ **c.** Ms. Martin went shopping with her children.

_____ **d.** The police took the man away.

_____ **e.** A man walked toward her while she was putting the groceries in the trunk.

_____ **f.** The man fell over a bag of groceries.

_____ **g.** The man grabbed her purse.

Pronunciation

Content and Function Words

In speaking, the content words of a sentence are stressed and the function words are usually unstressed.

Content Words			Function Words		
Nouns	flood	fire	*Pronouns*	he	him
Verbs	strike	hit	*Auxiliary Verbs*	is	do
Adjectives	awful	afraid	*Other Adjectives*	my	this
Adverbs	quickly	suddenly	*Articles*	the	a/an
Question Words	who	what	*Prepositions*	on	in
Negatives	no	didn't			

 3 Listen to the dialogue. The stressed words are in bold type. Practice saying the dialogue with a partner.

A: **What** was **Andy doing when** the **volcano erupted**?

B: He was **reading** a **novel**.

A: **What** did he **do when** the **fire started**?

B: He **jumped** into the **pool**.

 4 Read the dialogue. Predict which words are stressed by underlining the words. Then listen to the dialogue to check your predictions.

A: Can people predict earthquakes?

B: Not really, but in 1975 the Chinese predicted a 7.3 quake two days before it struck in the city of Haicheng.

A: Wow! 7.3! Was there a lot of damage?

B: Yes, it destroyed 90 percent of the buildings.

A: How did they know it was coming?

B: They noticed a series of minor quakes beforehand. They also saw changes in the water levels of the wells. And the animals were acting strangely.

A: That's amazing!

5 With a partner, practice reading the dialogue, focusing on word stress.

Speak Out

 Telling a Story When you tell a story, you can use certain expressions to show the sequence of events.

> It all began with ...
> First of all ...
> Then/After that ...
> Finally ...

 6 Have you ever had a close call? Was it an accident, a flood, a fire, a hurricane, or something else? Try to remember everything about it (e.g., time, place, people, your reactions and feelings). Work with a partner. Take turns telling your stories.

Read About It

 Before You Read

    a. What causes earthquakes?

    b. What happens during an earthquake?

 Making Predictions Before you read a text, you should try to predict what it is about. To do this, preview the reading by looking at the title, headings, and any pictures and captions that come with the text.

 Look at the title of the article and the picture. Predict the kinds of information you will find in the text. Make a list and share it with the class.

The San Francisco Earthquake of 1906

    The west coast of California is part of the Great Pacific Basin. More than 80 percent of the world's earthquakes occur in this area. In fact, California has about 1,000 earthquakes a year. Many of these
5 earthquakes are minor. They are so small that only animals and seismographs (machines that measure earthquakes) feel them. But about every 100 years, a major earthquake causes terrible losses of life and property. The famous San Francisco earthquake of
10 April 18, 1906, is an example.

    At 5:15 on that spring morning, a few people were waking up, getting dressed, having breakfast, waiting for streetcars, or walking to work, but most San Franciscans were sleeping when the ground began to shake. One of the first buildings to fall was the city hall. Damages to this building alone totaled $7 million. Thousands of other
15 buildings followed. Broken electric wires and gas lines started many fires. Broken streets and water lines made it impossible for firefighters to put out the fires. Within twenty-four hours, the city was destroyed. Over 28,000 buildings burned. About 2,500 people died and 250,000 lost their homes.

    One of the survivors was Enrico Caruso, the famous opera singer. When the
20 earthquake struck, he was staying at the Palace Hotel. The hotel's decorative glass dome shattered. Caruso escaped. He put a towel around his throat to protect his voice, grabbed his autographed picture of President Theodore Roosevelt, and ran out of the building.

    Architects and engineers rebuilt San Francisco. In three years, over 20,000
25 buildings were built. All of them were bigger, stronger, and safer than the ones that were destroyed. Many scientists believe that San Francisco will experience a much stronger earthquake before 2006, the year this hundred-year cycle ends. Will San Francisco be able to survive another huge earthquake?

3 Answer the questions.

    a. Where do about 80 percent of the world's earthquakes occur?

    b. Do people notice many of these earthquakes?

    c. What were most San Franciscans doing when the earthquake struck?

    d. When do scientists think there will be another major earthquake in San Francisco?

4 Use the context to guess the meanings of the words in the left column.

_____ **1.** to occur (line 3)	**a.** important
_____ **2.** minor (line 5)	**b.** to break into pieces
_____ **3.** major (line 8)	**c.** destruction
_____ **4.** losses (line 8)	**d.** to extinguish
_____ **5.** to put out (line 16)	**e.** a repeating period of time
_____ **6.** survivors (line 19)	**f.** to keep from danger
_____ **7.** to shatter (line 21)	**g.** people who had a close call
_____ **8.** to protect (line 21)	**h.** to take suddenly
_____ **9.** to grab (line 22)	**i.** to happen
_____ **10.** cycle (line 27)	**j.** not important

Think About It

5 Many people live in areas where dangerous events such as earthquakes and floods happen frequently. Why do people stay in these areas when they know about the danger?

6 Scientists have many instruments to help them get information about natural disasters such as earthquakes and volcanic eruptions. Do you think we will ever know enough to really control nature? Why or why not?

Write: The Concluding Sentence

A paragraph generally ends with a concluding sentence. This sentence pulls the paragraph together and tells the reader the paragraph is finished. The concluding sentence often restates the main idea in different words or summarizes the major points. It should follow naturally from the body of the paragraph.

7 Read the two paragraphs. For each, write a topic sentence on the line. Then check the best concluding sentence.

a.

_____.

First of all, I got to the train station late and I felt tired. Then, while I was waiting in line, a woman got ahead of me with her two screaming children. When I told her that I was first, she got angry and began shouting at me. Then, when I got on the train, I discovered that I had lost my ticket. When I got home, I was tired and angry.

☐ It was the last train ride I'll ever take.

☐ I take the train a lot.

b.

_____.

We were driving home when it started to rain. Suddenly, it began to rain harder and harder. In fact, it was raining so hard that we couldn't see anything. We were driving very slowly when we realized that the water was halfway up the side of the car.

☐ It was definitely a frightening experience.

☐ Tornadoes are dangerous too.

Write About It

8 Write a paragraph about a bad experience or a close call. Use time words in your story. Be sure you have a focused topic sentence, supporting sentences, and a concluding sentence.

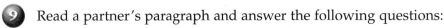

9 Read a partner's paragraph and answer the following questions:

  a. Do all the supporting sentences relate to the main idea?

  b. Are there any places where you would like additional information?

  c. Does the conclusion follow naturally from the body of the paragraph?

 10 **Check Your Writing** After getting feedback from your partner, revise your paragraph as necessary. Use the questions below.

> • Does the paragraph say what you want it to say?
> • Are time words used to signal the order of events?
> • Are verb tenses used correctly?

THE BEST IN LIFE

Unit 6

GETTING STARTED

Warm Up

1 We often find out about new products from advertisements or "ads." Think of one or two products you bought because of ads. Where did you see the ads? How did the ads persuade you to buy the products?

2 You are going to hear three radio ads. What product is each trying to sell? Write the letter of the ad on the line. There is one extra picture.

1. _____

2. _____

3. _____

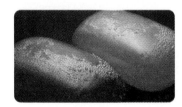

4. _____

Unit 6

53

Figure It Out

3 Describe your dream car. Is it a sports car or a luxury car? What special features does it have? Make a list. Compare your list with a partner's.

4 Look at the car in the ad below. What unusual features do you think the car has? Check the boxes.

- ☐ powerful engine
- ☐ bed
- ☐ stereo
- ☐ refrigerator
- ☐ TV

- ☐ telephone
- ☐ radio
- ☐ swimming pool
- ☐ microwave oven
- ☐ sauna

How much do you think this car costs? _____
How many drivers do you think it needs? _____

New From Luxury Motors!
The American Dream Car

Here is your chance to own the American Dream Car! You work hard to get the best things in life. Don't you deserve to have the very best car?

5 Now you can enjoy the most exciting car of your life—the American Dream! The American Dream is the longest, biggest, and most modern luxury car in the world.

10 The American Dream is the most comfortable car on the road! It is 60 feet (18.3 meters) long, and fifty of your closest friends can ride in it at the same time. Some of its special features 15 include a pool, a water bed, a refrigerator, a radio, ten telephones, three color TVs, a microwave oven, a stereo system, and more. It even has a landing pad for your helicopter!

The American Dream is the most 20 advanced, up-to-date car in the world. This amazing car has six wheels in front and ten wheels in back. The American Dream can go faster than any other car on the road. Its two 25 large, high-powered engines make it the most powerful car in the world. This car is so advanced that it needs two drivers, just like a jet plane!

The American Dream is the finest 30 car that you will ever own! Buy it for yourself or for your husband or wife. Luxury Motors will build an American Dream car for you for only $2 million.

Call your Luxury Motors salesperson 35 *right away and make an appointment today!*

5 Answer the questions.

   a. What are the main luxury features of the American Dream?

   b. What makes the American Dream the most powerful car in the world?

   c. Would you like to own a car like this? Why or why not?

   d. Is having an expensive car important for a person's "image"? Why or why not?

6 **Vocabulary Check** Match the words with the correct meaning.

_____ **1.** chance (line 1)	**a.**	ahead of others
_____ **2.** to own (line 1)	**b.**	machine that converts energy into motion
_____ **3.** to deserve (line 4)	**c.**	strong
_____ **4.** luxury (line 9)	**d.**	to have, possess
_____ **5.** features (line 14)	**e.**	now
_____ **6.** advanced (line 21)	**f.**	opportunity
_____ **7.** engine (line 26)	**g.**	characteristics, qualities
_____ **8.** powerful (line 27)	**h.**	to have the right to
_____ **9.** right away (line 36)	**i.**	a time to meet
_____ **10.** appointment (line 36)	**j.**	very comfortable and expensive

Talk About It

A Luxury Motors salesperson is trying to persuade a customer to buy an American Dream car. Look at their conversation.

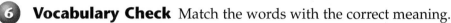

   State a feature.

A: I'm looking for a really big car.

   Persuade by describing the feature.

B: Then you'll like the American Dream. It's the biggest car in the world!

   Ask for proof.

A: Is it really the largest car in the world?

   Give proof.

B: Oh, yes. It's so big that you can land a helicopter on it.

7 With a partner, continue the conversation. The customer asks about:

a. length	**f.** power
b. comfort	**g.** speed
c. price	**h.** number of features
d. luxury	**i.** quality of engines
e. safety	**j.** reliability

The Superlative: Comparing Three or More Items

When we compare three or more items, we use the superlative form
of the adjective.

One-syllable adjectives: add **the –est**	The XE20 is **the fastest** computer in this store.
Two-syllable adjectives ending in **–y**: change **y** to **i** and add **the –est**	It is **the easiest** of all to use.
Adjectives with two or more syllables: use **the most** or **the least**	Naturally, the XE20 is **the most expensive**.
Exceptions: good → the best bad → the worst far → the farthest	But it's also **the best** computer on the market.

1 Complete the ad for Skyways with the superlative form of the
adjectives in parentheses.

Fly the best airline in the sky!

1. Fly _____ **(Good)** Airline in the Sky!

SKYWAYS is …

2. _____ **(safe)** of all airlines.
3. _____ **(friendly)** in the skies.
4. _____ **(reliable)** in the air.
5. _____ **(comfortable)** in the world.
6. It serves _____ **(good)** food!
7. And it's _____ **(expensive)** anywhere!

Fly **SKYWAYS!** The Way to Get There Fast!

② Complete the passage with the correct form of the adjectives in parentheses.

Advertising Signs

(a. enormous) _____ advertising sign in the world is in Kowloon, Hong Kong. It is 210 feet (64 meters) long and 55 feet (16.7 meters) high.

Every city in the world has signs telling people that they are entering the city, but the one in Hollywood, California is **(b. famous)** _____ in the world. It is in the hills above the city. Its letters are 30 feet (9 meters) wide and 45 feet (13.7 meters) tall.

(c. noticeable) _____ sign in the world was probably the Citroën sign on the Eiffel Tower. People could see it from as far as 24 miles (38.6 kilometers) away. It also had **(d. great)** _____ number of lightbulbs of any sign ever built, over 250,000. It was put up in 1925 and taken down in 1936.

(e. high) _____ sign in the world is on the top of a seventy-two-floor building in Toronto, Canada. It advertises a bank.

③ Give your opinion about the topics and then support your opinion.

Example: good/singer

In my opinion, Maria Bethania from Brazil is the best singer in the world because her voice is so beautiful.

a. beautiful/city	**d.** bad/habit	**g.** dangerous/sport
b. exciting/car	**e.** interesting/book	**h.** good/movie
c. nice/restaurant	**f.** enjoyable/music	**i.** idea of your own

④ Discuss your opinions with a partner. If you don't agree, give a reason. Use the model.

A: In my opinion, Garth Brooks is the best singer in the world.

B: I don't agree. I think Celine Dion is the best.

A: Really? Why do you think that?

B: She sings great songs in French and English.

Making Comparisons with Adverbs and Nouns

To form the comparative and superlative of adverbs, we use the same rules as for adjectives (see page 24).

> **Comparative**
> You know, the new XTR runs **faster** and **more efficiently than** the old XTR.
> **Superlative**
> Yes, in fact, it runs **the fastest** and **the most efficiently** of all computers on the market.

We can also use nouns in the comparative and superlative.

> **Comparative**
>
> The new XTR costs **less money** and has **more features than** the old one.
>
> **Superlative**
>
> And it uses **the least energy**, but has **the most power of** any computer on the market.

5 Complete the passage about Sam DuGood. Use the comparative or superlative form of the adjective, adverb, or noun in parentheses.

      Only one month ago, Sam DuGood was tired and overworked. He was **(a. productive)** _the least productive_ of all the secretaries in the office. But now, thanks to vitamins and healthy living, he's **(b. good)** _____ secretary in the office. He arrives at work **(c. early)** _____, stays **(d. late)** _____, and he has **(e. energy)** _____ of everyone. He does **(f. work)** _____ and has **(g. talent)** _____ any of the other secretaries. In fact, he's **(h. efficient)** _____ secretary in the company. Don't let Sam DuGood do **(i. good)** _____ you!

6 **Check Your Understanding** In which situations are you likely to use the superlative? Compare you answers with a partner's.

- [ ] Choosing one of several possible gifts to buy someone
- [ ] Describing a frightening experience in your life
- [ ] Refusing an invitation to a party
- [ ] Persuading your colleagues to give an award to a fellow colleague
- [ ] Deciding to go to college in your country or abroad

7 **Express Yourself** With a partner, choose one of the situations you checked above. Imagine yourselves in the situation and write a dialogue.

LISTENING and SPEAKING

Listen: Advertisements

1 **Before You Listen** Describe two or three ads that you like a lot. Why do you remember them? What were the ads trying to sell? Who were the advertisers trying to sell their product to?

STRATEGY **Listening to Draw Conclusions** When you listen, you can draw conclusions from information that is directly stated and from information that is not.

2 Listen to four different ads. What products are the ads trying to sell?

a. _____ b. _____ c. _____ d. _____

3 Advertisers try to sell their products to certain groups of people, such as adults, teenagers, children, or women. Listen to the ads again. Which group does each ad target?

a. _____ **b.** _____ **c.** _____ **d.** _____

4 Which of these products would you buy? Why? What information helped you draw your conclusions?

Pronunciation

> **Numbers: –*teen* vs. –*ty***
>
> The –*teen* numbers (e.g. fifteen) and the –*ty* numbers (e.g. fifty) have different stressed syllables.

 5 Pronounce each phrase after you hear it, and draw a line under the stressed syllable in each number.

a.	thir teen,	not	thir ty	pesos	
b.	four teen,	not	for ty	dollars	
c.	fif teen,	not	fif ty	escudos	
d.	six teen,	not	six ty	francs	
e.	seven teen,	not	seven ty	pesetas	
f.	eigh teen,	not	eigh ty	drachmas	

6 Which numbers have the stress on the first syllable? _____
Which numbers have the stress on the second syllable? _____

Speak Out

 Arguing, Counterarguing, Conceding In giving opinions, you use expressions to argue your point, to counterargue (argue back), and to concede (give in).

Arguing	Counterarguing	Conceding
I'm sure you agree that …	Yes, but …	Well, maybe you're right.
Don't forget that …	Well, I think that …	I agree.
Don't you think that …	Well, maybe but …	You have a point there.

7 Every year the Drexel Company gives $5,000 to the worker who works the hardest and is the most needy. Work in groups. Decide which of these workers deserves the money. Use comparatives, superlatives, and the expressions above.

> **Peter Rosen** is a secretary. He works ten to twelve hours a day and is never absent from work. He has three children and his wife is in the hospital. Her hospital care is very expensive, and they don't know how they are going to pay for it.

Rodolfo Sanchez is an electrician. Last month, he put out a fire that was going to burn down the company office building. He has two children, a son and a daughter. He doesn't make much money and says that he only has enough money to send one of the children to college.

Alice Kim is a computer scientist. She just wrote a new computer program that will earn the company millions of dollars. She earns a lot of money. However, she has to pay back the money she used to pay for her college education.

READING and WRITING

Read About It

 Before You Read

    a. What kind of information would you expect to find in an article about advertising? Make a list.

    b. How much money do you think U.S. companies spend on ads in a year? Write your prediction on the line. _____

 Noticing Examples When you read, you will understand more if you pay attention to examples that writers use to illustrate their ideas. Watch for expressions such as *for example, namely, that is,* and *for instance.* These signal that the writer is about to give an example.

The World of Advertising

    Advertising is probably as old as the products it persuades us to buy. The first advertisements were oral. People with something to sell shouted the name of
5 the product and its cost in the street for everyone to hear. For example, people sold animals and food in this way. Written ads developed early, too. For instance, an ad from Greece over 3,000
10 years old mentioned a shop with the best cloth, and in ancient Rome, ads announced circuses. In the Middle Ages, advertisers used drawings as most people did not know how to read. In the 1600s, after the invention of printing, ads began to appear in newspapers. Since the 1700s, advertising has become increasingly important.

15   In today's world, it is difficult to imagine what it would be like without the hundreds of ads we see and hear every day. Advertising has so much importance now that companies spend billions of dollars every year to call attention to their products. In 1997, for example, U.S. companies spent over $180 billion on advertising.

give power to your eyes

mistica K2350

The new K2350. Taking pictures. Higher.™ **mistica cameras**

20 Advertisers spend these huge sums of money because they know that ads are the most effective means of persuasion. The writers of the best ads use many different techniques to persuade the public. In some ads, for example, actors, sports stars, or singers recommend products. The advertiser hopes that the public will believe the person because he or she is famous. Another method focuses on the customers' emotions. These ads try to make people feel bad or guilty because they don't use

25 a certain product like a brand of cereal or a kind of detergent. Another method, the scientific approach, uses scientific test results to show that products work well.

Advertisers use all of these methods and many more in the hope that people will buy the newest, best, and most exciting product—theirs.

2 Answer the questions.

   a. When did printed ads first appear?

   b. Why do advertisers spend so much money on ads?

   c. What are two techniques that advertisers use to persuade buyers?

3 Use the context to match each word with its meaning.

_____ **1.**	oral (line 3)	**a.**	quantities
_____ **2.**	to announce (line 12)	**b.**	to get people to notice
_____ **3.**	drawings (line 12)	**c.**	to be seen in
_____ **4.**	to appear (line 14)	**d.**	way
_____ **5.**	to call attention to (line 17)	**e.**	to say something is good
_____ **6.**	sums (line 19)	**f.**	said or spoken
_____ **7.**	to recommend (line 22)	**g.**	pictures
_____ **8.**	method (line 25)	**h.**	to inform the public about

4 Scan the article for phrases that introduce examples and underline them. Then identify the example that each phrase introduces. Compare your answers with a partner's.

Think About It

5 Describe some of your favorite ads. Why do you like them? What techniques do they use?

6 Do you think it is right for advertisers to spend so much money on ads? Why or why not?

7 Is advertising honest? Explain your opinion.

Write: Ordering Supporting Sentences

One way to organize a paragraph is using chronological order. Another way to order supporting sentences is according to importance (from the most important to the least or from the least important to the most). This is called rank order. We use words and expressions such as *first of all, second, main,* and *most importantly* to show rank order.

8 In your opinion, what are the most important criteria? Rank the criteria from 1 (most important) to 5 (least important).

    a. Advantages of buying a new car:

        _____ low price   _____ comfortable seats   _____ nice color

        _____ large size   _____ powerful engine

    b. Advantages of buying a house:

        _____ many rooms   _____ large pool   _____ close to work, school

        _____ big yard   _____ friendly neighborhood

9 Read the sentences below. Write **T** in front of the topic sentence. Number the supporting sentences in order from 1 to 4. Write **C** in front of the concluding sentence.

    _____ **a.** When you get to California, rent your car from Honest Joe's Car Rental Service and visit California the right way!

    _____ **b.** There are many advantages to visiting California by car.

    _____ **c.** Also, most roads are toll free and in good condition.

    _____ **d.** However, the best reason of all is that public transportation is slow, inconvenient, expensive, or often unavailable.

    _____ **e.** Another advantage is that gasoline is cheap and available everywhere.

    _____ **f.** First of all, there is an extensive system of roads, which connects every point on the map.

10 How did you decide on the order of the sentences? Underline all the words and phrases that helped you order the sentences.

Write About It

11 Write a paragraph persuading your audience to buy a particular product or service. First, choose a product or service that you know well. Brainstorm and focus your ideas. Then write your paragraph. Include a topic sentence, at least five supporting sentences, and a concluding sentence. Use words that show order of importance.

12 **Check Your Writing** Exchange paragraphs with a partner. Use the questions below to suggest areas that need revision. Discuss your papers and revise as needed.

> • Is the paragraph persuasive?
>
> • Are the supporting sentences ranked by importance?
>
> • Are words used to signal the order of importance?

1 Complete the passage with the correct form of one of the verbs in the box. Use the simple past or past progressive tense.

buy	play
call	remember
dial	take
go out	pay

   Yesterday I **(1.)** _____ a new CD by Rock N. Roller and the Broken Bones Band. I **(2.)** _____ it home to listen to right away. While I **(3.)** _____ it, the electricity **(4.)** _____ . I **(5.)** _____ the electric company to complain, but as I **(6.)** _____ their number, I **(7.)** _____ I **(8. neg.)** _____ the bill last month!

2 Complete the conversation with the correct form of the verbs in parentheses. Use the simple past or past progressive tense.

KIM: Hey, Pam. I **(1. try)** _____ to call you last night, but your line **(2. be)** _____ busy.

PAM: Hi, Kim. I know. I'm sorry.

KIM: **(3. talk)** _____ you _____ to your boyfriend?

PAM: No. I **(4. use)** _____ my computer. I **(5. be)** _____ on the Internet.

KIM: Oh. **(6. work)** _____ you _____ on your project for history class?

PAM: No. I **(7. listen)** _____ to a live interview with the Broken Bones Band.

KIM: Really? I just **(8. get)** _____ their new CD. I really like it.

3 Complete the paragraph with an appropriate time expression from the box.

after	then
finally	when
soon	while

   Last night was Rock N. Roller's big concert. **(1.)** _____ Rock N. Roller finished singing, he smashed his guitar on stage. Karen was watching Rock on stage **(2.)** _____ a piece of his guitar hit her on the head. Karen didn't think she was hurt, but **(3.)** _____ she noticed she had a lump on her head, so she went to the first aid station. **(4.)** _____ she was waiting at the first aid station, a reporter took her picture. An article about Karen **(5.)** _____ appeared in the local paper. Karen saved that piece of Rock's guitar for a while, but she **(6.)** _____ sold it to a rock and roll collector for several hundred dollars!

4 Complete the paragraph with the correct form of the adjectives in parentheses.

And now, here's the weather. As you listeners know, a tornado struck Park City Airport yesterday morning. Since then, two more tornadoes have done damage in the area. The last of the three was **(1. serious)** _____. It lasted **(2. long)** _____ and caused **(3. great)** _____ damage. Local business owners say that this tornado was **(4. bad)** _____ in the area's history. The mayor, however, has good news. Park City will receive **(5. large)** _____ share of money from the state's emergency relief fund. And now, back to our music. Here's **(6. popular)** _____ song from Will Smith's new CD.

5 Write sentences comparing the three vases of flowers. Use comparative and superlative forms of adjectives in the box.

elegant	large
expensive	simple
good	pretty

a. _____

b. _____

c. _____

d. _____

e. _____

Vocabulary Review

Use the words in the box to complete the sentences.

advertising	luxury
damage	performance
deserve	power
feature	survivors
height	talent

1. The American Dream car is the biggest _____ car in the world.

2. Celine Dion's _____ of her hit song was wonderful!

3. The flood caused eight million dollars' worth of _____ to the area.

4. Many international companies spend millions of dollars on _____.

5. The _____ I like the best about the American Dream car is the swimming pool!

6. The _____ of the plane crash waited two days before help came.

7. Ben and Betty _____ the award because they worked the hardest.

8. My cousin has real _____ as a country singer; you should hear her.

GETTING STARTED

Warm Up

1 What kinds of information do employers want to find out during job interviews? How can you best get ready for a job interview? Make a list of answers for each question.

2 Listen to the conversations. What information is the employer trying to find out from each job applicant? Write the number of the conversation in the correct box.

- ☐ education
- ☐ reason for leaving last job
- ☐ present salary
- ☐ number of years at last job
- ☐ experience

Figure It Out

Discoveries magazine is looking for a reporter to travel all over the world and write adventure articles. Ms. Tyler is interviewing Cristina Vela for the job.

A. **MS. TYLER:** So, Ms. Vela, you're interested in working for *Discoveries?*

CRISTINA: That's right. I've written lots of articles for newspapers.

MS. TYLER: Oh? What newspapers have you worked for?

CRISTINA: Well, I've sold articles to the *New Kensington Star* and a few other newspapers.

MS. TYLER: Have you ever written an adventure article?

CRISTINA: No, I haven't, but I've done some adventurous things to get information for my articles. I've even taken risks.

MS. TYLER: Tell me about one of them.

CRISTINA: Well, once I wanted to report on prisons, so I stole something from a store. I spent five days in prison. It was horrible, but later I wrote an article about my experiences there. When the public read the article, they were upset and complained. Since then, the prisons have really improved.

MS. TYLER: That certainly is interesting and adventuresome.

B. **MS. TYLER:** And how long have you been a reporter for the *Star?*

CRISTINA: Since last July … so, for about a year.

MS. TYLER: And why are you applying for a job with us?

CRISTINA: Because I'd like to work abroad. I've never crossed the Atlantic.

MS. TYLER: Have you ever been up the Amazon River?

CRISTINA: No, I haven't, but I'd love to go. I've always dreamed about doing a story on the rain forests.

MS. TYLER: Well, Ms. Vela, I like your enthusiasm. I think you'd be perfect for the job. When can you start?

3 Answer the questions.

a. What kind of person is *Discoveries* magazine looking for?

b. What experience does Cristina Vela have?

c. How did Cristina get information for her article on the prison?

d. Do you think Cristina Vela is right for the job? Why or why not? Would you want this job?

e. People have different criteria for choosing a job, such as money or flexible work hours. What criteria are important to you?

4 **Vocabulary Check** Match the words with their meanings.

_____ **1.** employer   **a.** boss

_____ **2.** salary   **b.** to do things that can be dangerous

_____ **3.** to take risks   **c.** unhappy and angry

_____ **4.** to upset   **d.** to say bad things about

_____ **5.** to complain   **e.** interest, excitement

_____ **6.** enthusiasm   **f.** money paid for work

Talk About It

 5 With a partner, take turns being an employer and a job applicant. Ask and answer questions using the cues.

Example:

job: reporter

experience: writes articles for the *Herald*/a year

State job and ask about past experience.

A: I see you want a job as a reporter. What kind of experience have you had?

Tell experience.

B: Well, I've written several articles for the *Herald*.

Ask about length of time.

A: And how long have you worked at the *Herald*?

Tell length of time.

B: For about a year.

a. **job:** history teacher   **experience:** teaches at Valley High School/September 1989

b. **job:** computer technician   **experience:** fixes computers for Unex/last March

c. **job:** store clerk   **experience:** sells records at Cactus Records/five years

d. **job:** tennis teacher   **experience:** works for Atlas Health Club/five months

e. **job:** waiter   **experience:** works at Maxim's Restaurant/August 1996

GRAMMAR

The Present Perfect: Relating the Past to the Present

We use the present perfect tense (*have*/*has* + past participle) to talk about an action that happened sometime in the past, but is still relevant in the present. This use is often signaled by time words such as *before, ever, so far, up to now, always,* and *never.*

> **A:** **Have** you ever **worked** as a journalist?
>
> **B:** I**'ve** never **worked** for a daily, but last year the local newspaper published one of my stories.
>
> **A:** Really? What other kinds of stories **have** you **written**?
>
> **B:** So far, I**'ve** only **written** this one.

1 Many common verbs have irregular past participles. Complete the chart with the past participles.

is	was	_____	do	did	_____	begin	began	_____
have	had	_____	take	took	_____	get	got	_____
go	went	_____	make	made	_____	see	saw	_____
write	wrote	_____	come	came	_____	meet	met	_____

2 Melanie Gibson is interviewing Indira Jones for a job as a guide. Write the correct form of the verb on the line.

MELANIE: So, Indira, you want to be an adventure guide in the Andes.

INDIRA: Yes, Ms. Gibson, I **(1. always, love)** _____ the Andes.

MELANIE: And **(2. you, ever, work)** _____ as an adventure guide before?

INDIRA: Yes, so far I **(3. take)** _____ a group of grandmothers on a white-water raft trip in Colorado. And two years ago, I **(4. cross)** _____ a 16,000-foot mountain pass in Nepal with a group of teens … in the winter.

MELANIE: Impressive, but the Andes are different. **(5. you, study)** _____ to be a guide?

INDIRA: Well, last summer I **(6. take)** _____ a course in outdoor survival. They **(7. teach)** _____ us about outdoor medical emergencies. But generally, in my life, I **(8. learn)** _____ most from hands-on experience.

MELANIE: Well, Indira, you sound like the perfect guide for an adventure trip to Machu Pichu.

The Present Perfect: Repeated Past Actions

The present perfect tense also expresses an action that has repeated at unspecified times in the past. To ask questions, we use *How many* or *How often*.

> **A:** How many adventure stories **have** you **written** so far?
>
> **B:** Well, up to now, I**'ve finished** four, but I'm working on another now.
>
> **A:** How often **have** you **had** a close call on these trips?
>
> **B:** Only four times. I**'ve had** good luck.

3 With a partner, take turns asking about your life experiences. Ask questions with *How many times* or *How often*.

Example: fly an airplane

A: How many times have you flown in an airplane?

B: Up to now, I've flown four times. *or* I've never flown before.

a. travel abroad		**e.** fall in love
b. attend a concert		**f.** fall asleep in class
c. have a close call		**g.** lose something important
d. use the Internet		**h.** idea of your own

The Present Perfect Tense with *How long*

We use the present perfect tense to talk about an action that began in the past and continues up to the present moment. To ask about the length of time, we use *How long*, and we generally answer with *for* or *since*.

> **A:** So, how long **have** you **taken** pictures of famous people?
>
> **B:** I**'ve photographed** famous people ever **since** I graduated from school.
>
> **A:** And how long **have** you **worked** as a freelance journalist?
>
> **B:** I**'ve been** a reporter **for** about three years now.

4 Match each sentence with its meaning. Write the letter on the line.

_____ **1.** He has worked as a nurse for two years.

_____ **2.** He worked as a nurse for two years.

    a. He worked as a nurse for two years, but isn't doing this job now.

    b. He began working as a nurse two years ago, and is still a nurse.

_____ **3.** How long did you live in Mexico City?

_____ **4.** How long have you lived in Mexico City?

    a. You don't live in Mexico City now.

    b. You live in Mexico City now.

5 **Check Your Understanding** In which situations are you likely to use the present perfect tense? Check your answers with a partner's.

☐ Giving your boss or teacher an update on a project

☐ Inviting a friend to your house for lunch

☐ Interviewing a person about his travel experiences abroad

☐ Asking a friend for her opinion about a movie

☐ Asking a person about the length of time at your school

With your partner, choose one of the situations you checked. Imagine yourselves in the situation and write a dialogue.

6 **Express Yourself** Walk around the room and find someone who has done each of the activities listed below. When you find someone, continue the conversation by asking a follow-up question.

Example: travel abroad

A: Have you ever traveled abroad?	**A:** Have you ever traveled abroad?
B: Yes, I have. I went abroad last year.	**B:** Unfortunately, I haven't.
A: Where did you go?	
B: I went to Cairo.	

a. take music lessons
b. go to a live concert
c. be in a car accident
d. surf the Internet
e. apply for a job
f. go scuba diving
g. see a famous person
h. be in the hospital
i. idea of your own

LISTENING and SPEAKING

Listen: A Job Interview

 Before You Listen

a. What are some of the jobs people do to make a movie?
b. What does a stuntman do? List some examples.

STRATEGY **Understanding Grammar Clues** You understand more if you listen for grammar clues, like word endings and auxiliary verbs. These clues signal such aspects as singular and plural, or present, past, and future time frames.

  A stuntman is interviewing for a job. Listen and complete the chart.

Name:	*Hal Hunk*
Length of time as a stuntperson:	
First stunt:	
Age:	
Stunt experience:	*has driven cars and motorcycles*
Most recent stunt:	
Stunts never tried:	

Pronunciation

> **Sentence Stress**
>
> In every thought group, a group of words that expresses a thought, the last content word is usually stressed more than the others. The stressed syllable of this word is called sentence stress. Other content words are less stressed.

 3 Listen to the dialogue. The syllable in bold carries the sentence stress.

    A: /For a **year** now,/Ms. Holmes has been **may**or./What's she accomplished so **far**?/

    B: /She's hired fifty new po**lice** officers./

4 Read the dialogue. For each thought group, predict which words carry the sentence stress and underline them.

    A: /And so,/what has Ms. Holmes done about crime?/

    B: /She's done a lot./ While she's been mayor,/crime has decreased by half./

    A: /That's amazing!/ What else has she done?/

    B: /She's made bicycle lanes all over the city/and closed several streets to traffic./

    A: /All in one year!/ I can't wait to see what's next./

Now listen to the dialogue and check your answers with the class. Then practice the dialogue with a partner, focusing on the correct sentence stress.

Speak Out

STRATEGY ▶ **Making Generalizations** When you want to make general statements that are true most of the time, use these expressions.

In most cases, …	Most people have …	Generally speaking, …
People usually …	In general, …	Most people now believe …

5 With two other students, discuss these questions.

    a. What jobs do men usually have in your country today? What jobs do women usually have in your country today?

    b. In your country, have traditional jobs for men and women changed in the last fifty years? Why or why not? How do you feel about this?

Read About It

1 **Before You Read** What skills do you think a newspaper reporter should have? Check your top three choices. Compare your answers with a partner's.

- ☐ solving problems
- ☐ getting along with people
- ☐ thinking quickly
- ☐ giving opinions
- ☐ organizing meetings

- ☐ listening carefully
- ☐ writing clearly
- ☐ interviewing
- ☐ taking notes
- ☐ meeting deadlines

Nellie Bly, Newspaperwoman

Elizabeth Cochrane, known as Nellie Bly, was an exceptional woman who worked to make life better for everybody. When she was about eighteen years old, she read an article in the *Pittsburgh*
5   *Dispatch* that spoke out against women. She was very upset, so she wrote a letter called "What Girls Are Good For" to the editor. This letter impressed the editors and they gave her a job.

Bly's career with the *Dispatch* began with a
10 series of articles about divorce. The public reacted very strongly for or against her articles. The editors, however, were surprised because they never believed that a young woman could write such controversial stories.

15 Bly's next articles were about the lives of the women who lived in boarding houses in Pittsburgh. Then she wrote about poor sections of the city, about employees in shops who worked long hours for low salaries, and about conditions in the prisons.

20 After Bly moved to New York City, Joseph Pulitzer, a famous newspaperman, asked her to write about conditions in mental hospitals for his paper, the *New York World*. She pretended to be crazy and within twenty-four hours, she was in a mental hospital. After ten days, she returned with stories about violent nurses, terrible food, and unsanitary conditions. These
25 stories were again controversial, but helped to improve hospital conditions.

This success encouraged Bly to write other stories. She jumped off a boat into the Hudson River so she could write a story about the rescue crew. She got herself arrested and spent time in prison. Her stories about prison conditions forced the authorities to separate men and women prisoners.

30   Because of a popular novel at the time, *Around the World in Eighty Days*, by Jules Verne, Bly decided she would travel around the world in fewer than eighty days. When Pulitzer wanted to send a man instead, her response was quick. "If you do," she said, "I'll leave at the same time and race against him!"

35   Pulitzer finally gave in, and she left New York on November 14, 1889. She crossed the Atlantic, interviewed Jules Verne in Paris, and traveled through the Suez, Somalia, Calcutta, Singapore, Yokohama, and San Francisco. Her readers followed her trip closely. When she arrived in New York, the whole city was amazed. She had made the trip in seventy-two days, six hours and
40 ten minutes.

     Bly continued to write stories after her journey, but she never again achieved the popularity she once had. She died in 1922 of pneumonia, at the age of fifty-five.

2   Find these words in the article and use the context to determine their meanings. Write short definitions on a sheet of paper. Work without a dictionary. Discuss your answers with the class.

a. impressed (line 7)	**e.** success (line 26)	**i.** gave in (line 35)
b. controversial (line 14)	**f.** authorities (line 28)	**j.** followed (line 38)
c. pretended (line 22)	**g.** instead (line 33)	**k.** achieved (line 41)
d. crazy (line 23)	**h.** response (line 33)	**l.** popularity (line 41)

 Making Inferences You can often figure out the writer's opinions or ideas even if they are not directly stated. You do this with other information in the text. In other words, you make inferences based on what you read.

3   Read each sentence and decide if the inference is one the text supports or one the text does not support. Write *yes* or *no*.

_____ **a.** Bly never got married.

_____ **b.** Conditions in mental hospitals were very bad.

_____ **c.** Pulitzer thought Bly was a good reporter.

_____ **d.** Pulitzer thought Bly was too young to go on a trip around the world.

_____ **e.** Bly was sure she could beat a man in a race around the world.

Think About It

4   Do you think the methods Nellie used to get information for her articles were fair? Why or why not?

5   Do you think Nellie faced unnecessary difficulties because she was a woman? Give examples.

6   What inferences can you draw about Nellie's personality?

Write: Supporting Details

In a well-developed paragraph, the supporting sentences are explained with supporting details. These details (facts, examples, experience, description) give specific information about each supporting point.

 7 Read the paragraph and complete the outline.

I believe Sarah Lewis is the best candidate for the position of English Instructor at Miles College. Ms. Lewis comes to the department with excellent credentials. First, she has a strong educational background. She holds two master's degrees, one in communication studies and one in linguistics. She also has a wide range of experience. She has taught in a refugee program in Indonesia, in a business program in Turkey, and in a university program in California. Finally, Ms. Lewis is truly professional and well respected. She has written several articles and presented at conferences. Her colleagues and students comment on how hard she works for her classes and the program. I am certain that Ms. Lewis will make a lasting contribution to our teaching staff.

Outline

Topic Sentence (Main Idea): *I believe Sarah Lewis is the best candidate for the position of English Instructor at Miles College.*

Supporting Point 1:   *Has a strong educational background*

    Detail 1:   *MA in communication studies*

    Detail 2:   *MA in linguistics*

Supporting Point 2: _____

    Detail 1: _____

    Detail 2: _____

    Detail 3: _____

Supporting Point 3: _____

    Detail 1: _____

    Detail 2: _____

    Detail 3: _____

Write About It

 8 Your boss asked you to find a new employee. You interviewed several people and chose one of them. Write a one-paragraph report to your boss explaining your choice. First, choose a specific job. Then give the person you selected a name. Write a paragraph explaining why the person is a match. Talk about the person's education, experience, and personality.

  9 **Check Your Writing** Reread your paragraph. Use the questions below and revise your paper as necessary.

- Are the supporting sentences ordered logically?
- Are the supporting points explained with details?
- Are verb tenses used correctly?

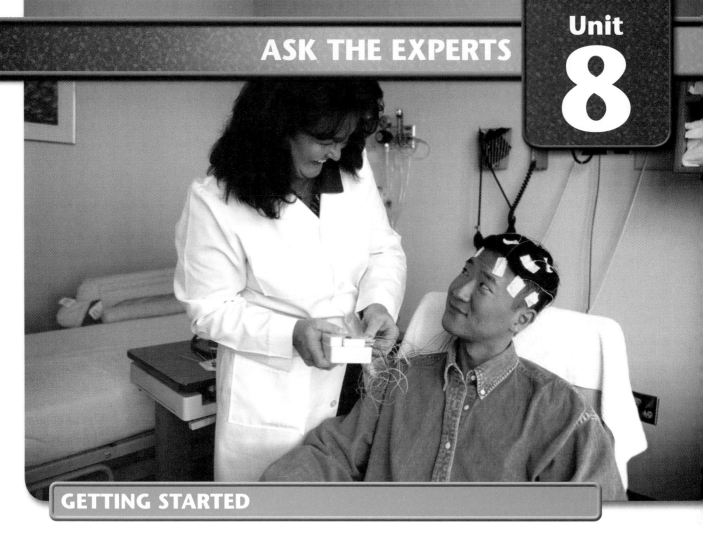

GETTING STARTED

Warm Up

1 We all have problems during our lives such as problems with our health or problems with our family. What other problems can people have? Make a list.

2 You are going to hear three conversations. What kind of problem is each person having? Write the letter of the conversation.

☐ health problem
☐ work problem
☐ school problem
☐ family problem

3 When you have a problem, who do you ask for advice?

Figure It Out

4 "Ask Andy Summers" is an advice column in the newspaper. People with problems write to Andy Summers and he responds with advice. On the next page, match the problem with the advice by writing the letter on the line.

Problem

_____**1.** My teacher is taking my class on a trip to England. All of my friends are going, but my parents say that I'm too young to travel abroad. I'm seventeen years old, but my parents think that I'm still a baby! What should I do?

_____**2.** My best friend always borrows money from me and never pays me back. Last month, he asked me for $500. Now he says that if I give him another $500, he'll be able to pay me back everything he owes me next July. Do you think I should believe him?

_____**3.** My husband and I both make good salaries, but he spends money as if we were millionaires! He shops all of the time and he always pays by credit card. Now we have no money at all and we owe thousands of dollars. What advice can you give me?

_____**4.** My son loves loud rock music. I can't stand rock, so one day I threw all his CDs away. Now he won't speak to me. What do you think I ought to do?

_____**5.** Last summer thieves broke into our house while we were on vacation and took everything. This year my husband refuses to go on vacation because he's afraid it'll happen again. I don't want to stay home all summer. What should I do?

_____**6.** I asked my boss for more money, but she refused. She said that I'm always late and take too many coffee breaks. I want a new job with a better boss. My friends say that I'd better not leave my job right away. What do you think?

_____**7.** On my last vacation, I gained a lot of weight. Now my clothes are too tight and I can't stop eating. Can you give me some advice?

_____**8.** My son and his wife have three beautiful children. The trouble is that they want me to watch their children while they're at work. I love my grandchildren, but I don't like watching them every day. What should I do?

Advice

a. I think your friend may not be able to return your money. Maybe you should find a new friend.

b. I agree with your friends. It sounds like you're not a very good worker. You'd better not quit the job you have now. In fact, you'd better work harder if you want to keep your job.

c. I advise you to go on vacation alone. Leave your husband at home to watch your house.

d. I think people like your husband shouldn't have credit cards. You should cut his credit cards in half and throw them away.

e. You should go on a diet. Don't eat candy or desserts. You ought to start exercising more, too. Join a health club and go there every day.

f. I think you ought to tell them that you're too busy to babysit.

g. You ought to apologize to your son. You should probably offer to buy him some new CDs, too.

h. You should ask them to consult with your teacher. Then they'll find out that you'll be with your teacher and your friends.

 5 Look at the problems and the advice again. Do you agree or disagree with the advice? Why? If you disagree, can you think of better advice?

6 Vocabulary Check Fill in the blanks with the correct words from the box.

owe	advised
can't stand	consult
borrowed	thief
salary	refuse

a. Clyde _____ my favorite CD yesterday. He says that he'll return it on Friday.

b. Tom says his neighbors are too noisy. He asked me what he should do. I _____ him to move.

c. I want to buy a computer, but I don't know much about them. I want to _____ with a computer expert first.

d. I _____ my roommate's bad habits.

e. A _____ grabbed my purse and ran away. He got all of my money and credit cards.

f. I don't make enough money. My boss ought to raise my _____.

Talk About It

7 *Help Line* is an advice hot line. People with problems call in and ask for advice. With a partner, take turns being the adviser and the caller. Use the cues.

Example: Your phone bill is too high.

Explain problem; ask for advice.

A: The phone company says that I made thirty calls to Australia last month, but I don't even know anyone in Australia! They're going to turn off my phone if I don't pay. What should I do?

Give advice.

B: You should call the phone company and complain.

Reject advice.

A: I don't think that'll work.

Give advice.

B: Well, maybe you should write a letter to the phone company and explain the situation.

Accept advice.

A: That's probably a better idea.

a. Your neighbors are noisy at night.
b. Someone in your family is a couch potato.
c. You don't know how to use your new computer.
d. Someone owes you a lot of money.
e. Your new bike doesn't work right.
f. You don't like your boss.
g. You can't stop smoking.
h. Idea of your own.

```
International Long Distance
TCT Calling Plan from 212-555-5555

No.  Date    Time      Place       Area-Number    *   Min.   Amount
1    Jan 08  05:48PM   AUSTRALIA   0613784293     S   45     21.60
2    Jan 13  08:23PM   AUSTRALIA   0614942217     X   32     15.36
3    Jan 13  08:24PM   AUSTRALIA   0618934392     X   24     11.52
4    Jan 14  06:06PM   AUSTRALIA   0616843470     S   54     25.92
Total TCT Calling Plan calls from 212-555-5555:         74.40

Total International Long Distance                        74.40
```

Giving Advice: *Should, Ought to*

To ask for and give advice, we can use the modals *should* or *ought to*.

> **A:** How **should** I **tell** my boss I'm looking for another job?
>
> **B:** You **shouldn't say** anything. You **should wait** till you have another job.
>
> **A:** I don't know. I think I really **ought to say** something now.

  1 **Check Your Understanding** Read the letter to Andy Summers. Then complete Andy's answer with *should, shouldn't,* or *ought*.

July 15

Dear Andy Summers,

My wife and I have been married for only a few weeks but we are having a lot of problems. We love each other but we have very different lifestyles. I like to get up late and she likes to get up early. She likes to go to the theater but I like to watch TV. She likes to go to fancy restaurants but I like pizza and hamburgers. I like to listen to rock music but she only likes classical music. We love each other a lot but we are driving each other crazy. I'm afraid that if we don't solve our problems, we are going to break up. What should we do?

Sincerely,

In Love But Not Happy

July 25

Dear In Love,

It's good to hear that with all of your problems, you are still in love. To solve your problems, you and your wife **(1.)**_____ to have a talk. You **(2.)**_____ agree to get up a little earlier and your wife **(3.)**_____ to agree to get up a little later. You **(4.)**_____ go to the movies with your wife once in a while and she **(5.)**_____ to stay home with you and watch TV once in a while, too. You **(6.)**_____ eat pizzas and hamburgers all of the time. This food is bad for your health. Also, you and your wife **(7.)**_____ find some restaurants that you both like. You **(8.)**_____ listen to rock music all of the time. No one can relax when rock music is playing. Maybe you **(9.)**_____ to throw away your rock albums and start listening to classical music.

Sincerely,

Andy Summers

Giving a Warning: *Had better*

When we want to give strong advice or a warning, we use *had better / had better not* + verb.

> **A:** I still think I should tell my boss I'm looking for another job.
>
> **B:** You**'d better take** my advice. You**'d better not tell** him, or you might not have a job at all!

2 In which situation might you say each of the following statements? Discuss your answers with a partner.

a. You'd better leave it alone.

b. You'd better not tell anyone.

c. I'd better go study.

d. You'd better not drink that.

e. He'd better apologize

f. We'd better not take the car.

Softening Advice

We often use *think* when we ask for or give advice with *should, ought to,* or *had better*. This makes the advice "softer."

> **SON:** **Do** you **think** I **should take** my credit card on my trip?
>
> **DAD:** Yes, and I **think** you **ought to hide** your money in your shoe!
>
> **SON:** Dad, **don't** you **think** you **should relax** a little?

3 Rewrite the dialogue. Use *I think, I don't think,* or *Do you think* in the numbered sentences.

A: I'm taking a trip to California. **(1.)** Should I visit San Francisco?

B: Yes, it's really beautiful! **(2.)** You ought to go to Los Angeles, too.

A: I hear that it's really warm in California. I can leave all my winter clothes at home!

B: Not really! It can get cold in San Francisco in the summer. **(3.)** You had better take some warm clothes with you.

A: OK. What about hotels? **(4.)** Should I stay at the West Hollywood Hotel in Los Angeles?

B: **(5.)** You shouldn't stay there. It's too expensive.

4 Consider the situations. For each, give advice with *should* or a warning with *had better / had better not*.

a. Anna loves to play volleyball. There is a new gym near her home.

b. The doctor says you're too thin. If you lose more weight, you will probably get sick.

c. That part of the city is dangerous! If you go there at night, be careful.

d. I read a wonderful book recently. I think you'd like it, too.

e. Put that medicine where the kids can't reach it.

f. Paolo is writing a paragraph and he doesn't know how to spell some words.

5 Work with a partner. Look at the pictures. Take turns asking for and giving advice, using a form of *think*.

a.

b.

c.

d.

e.

f.

Example:

A: What do you think he should do?

B: I think he ought to do the dishes.

 6 **Check Your Understanding** In which situations are you likely to use *should*, *ought to*, or *had better*? Check your answers with a partner's.

☐ Recommending a vacation spot to a friend

☐ Telling a friend how to get a driver's license

☐ Making an appointment to see a dentist

☐ Discussing a problem you have with a friend

☐ Comparing your health club with a friend's

 7 **Express Yourself** With a partner, choose one of the situations you checked above. Imagine yourselves in the situation and write a dialogue using different expressions of advice.

LISTENING and SPEAKING

Listen: *Ask Olga!*

1 **Before You Listen** Many radio and TV programs offer advice. People call on the phone and describe their problems, and listeners call in to give them advice. Why do you think that people ask for advice on these programs? Why do you think people call in to give advice?

STRATEGY **Listening for the Main Idea** You can understand more easily when you focus on getting the main idea of a conversation. Listen for key words or phrases that are repeated or stressed.

2 Listen to the radio program *Ask Olga!* What kind of problem is each person asking about? Check your answer.

Problem 1
- ☐ a problem with money
- ☐ a personal problem
- ☐ a problem at school

Problem 2
- ☐ a problem with someone at work
- ☐ a problem with something he borrowed
- ☐ a problem with something he bought

3 Listen to the program again. Complete the chart.

Problem 1	Advice 1	Advice 2
	She should get married.	

Problem 2	Advice 1	Advice 2
		He should go to the Better Business Bureau.

Pronunciation

Intonation Patterns

Yes/no questions have a rising intonation pattern.

Should we go alone?

Statements and information questions have a rising-falling intonation pattern.

No, you should ask Jonathan.

Why should I do that?

4 Circle the intonation you hear.

- **a.** rising   rising/falling
- **b.** rising   rising/falling
- **c.** rising   rising/falling
- **d.** rising   rising/falling
- **e.** rising   rising/falling
- **f.** rising   rising/falling
- **g.** rising   rising/falling
- **h.** rising   rising/falling
- **i.** rising   rising/falling
- **j.** rising   rising/falling

Speak Out

STRATEGY **Asking for and Giving Advice** When solving problems, you ask for and give advice. Sometimes you agree with people's advice and sometimes you don't.

Asking for Advice	Giving Advice
What do you think ... Do you think they should ... Should they ...	I think they should ... They ought to ... In my opinion, they'd better ...

5 Your city has received a large amount of money to solve one of its problems. Work in groups of three. Each student should read a different problem and then explain the problem to the group. As a group, decide which problem the city should spend the money on. Ask for advice and give advice.

a. In some neighborhoods, there are many thieves, and people are afraid to go out at night. Sometimes the thieves hurt or kill people to get their money. The city needs more police officers.

b. People are worried about the traffic problem. More and more people have cars. There are terrible traffic jams. Sometimes traffic stops completely. The city needs to build wider streets and new roads.

c. People are upset about the amount of air pollution in the city. Factories put huge quantities of smoke in the air. Cars, trucks, and buses add more pollution. If the city tells the companies to put in pollution controls, many factories will close. The city needs to help the factories pay for pollution controls.

READING and WRITING

Read About It

1 **Before You Read** In the past, people usually got advice from their families and friends. What are some different ways of getting advice today?

STRATEGY **Skimming** Before reading a text, it is a good idea to get a general idea of what the text is about. Skim, or read quickly, to find the main ideas.

2 Quickly skim the text. What is the main idea of paragraph one? Of paragraph two? Compare your answers with a partner's.

Help Is Out There

In the past, when people had problems, they went to relatives or friends to get advice. Today, thanks to technology, it is possible to get advice from radio shows, TV programs, telephone hot
5 lines, and the Internet.

Advice is everywhere. Listeners across the United States can call up radio programs to talk about their problems and get or give advice on the air. For example, the popular radio show *Car Talk*
10 gives advice on problems listeners are having with their cars. TV viewers can watch as people tell their life stories and describe their difficulties on many well-known talk shows such as *Sally Jesse Raphael* or *The Oprah Winfrey Show*.

Frequently, audience members on these shows make comments
15 and give their own advice to the talk-show guests. Other people with problems can dial telephone hot lines, specialized services that offer immediate access to advice
20 counselors. Callers may get advice on what to do about a snakebite, how to cook low-fat meals, or even how to solve a homework problem. But by far the fastest growing
25 source of advice and help is the Internet, a system of connected computers around the world that provides rapid access to many kinds of information.

30   There are several ways to give and get advice on the Internet. Computer users may join
a newsgroup, a kind of electronic discussion group that focuses on one subject.
For example, people with diabetes may join a group to read articles on how to deal
35 with this chronic disease, while people interested in improving their golf game can join
a newsgroup specializing in golf. Another way to get advice on the Internet is through
chatting, one of the Net's most popular features. In text-based chatting, people
communicate instantly in real time by typing messages back and forth. In multimedia
chat, people can have voice conversations and live video communication. Yet another
40 way to get advice or solve a problem is through visiting Web sites.

Web sites are collections of documents that may have text, images, sound, and
video. Each Web site has its own electronic address. For example, if students want
to check English grammar, they can visit the following address:
http://www.hiway.co.uk/~ei/intro.html.

45   To sum up, it is clear that technological advances today have given people many
more ways to give advice, get advice, and solve their problems.

3 In your own words, define the computer terms in the box. Share your definitions with the class.

> Internet
> chatting
> newsgroup
> Web site

4 Use the context to guess the meaning of the following words. Write your answers on a sheet of paper.

- **a.** difficulties (line 11)
- **b.** counselors (line 20)
- **c.** source (line 25)
- **d.** rapid (line 28)
- **e.** diabetes (line 34)
- **f.** Net (line 37)

5 What clue words in the context helped you figure out the meaning of each word? Compare your words with a partner's.

Think About It

6 Is it easier to get advice from a friend or from a stranger? Why?

7 Can you trust advice you find on the Internet? How do you know?

8 What experience have you had using the Internet? Have you ever asked for advice or solved a problem using the Internet? Explain.

Write: An Informal Letter

We send informal letters to family members, friends, and people we do not have important business relationships with. An informal letter has several standard parts: the date, the greeting, the body, the closing, and the signature.

9 Look at the letter to Andy Summers on page 78. Use it to answer the questions.

   a. Where do we put the date on a letter? The greeting? The closing? Where do we write the first line of a letter?

   b. How did the writer order the information in the letter? Write 1 to 3.

   _____ request for advice

   _____ identification of the problem

   _____ explanation of the problem

Write About it

10 You need some advice. Write a letter to Andy Summers. First, choose a problem. (For example, maybe you got a bad grade, you need money, or you don't like your job.) Brainstorm and focus your ideas. Then write a letter. Make sure that your letter identifies the problem, explains the problem, and requests advice. Don't forget to include the date, a greeting, and a closing. Use the letter on page 78 as an example.

☑ 11 Check Your Writing Exchange papers with a partner. Read your partner's letter, and using the questions below, suggest ways to improve the letter.

   - Are the parts of the letter easy to identify?
   - Is the problem identified in the first sentence?
   - Is the problem explained well?
   - Does the writer ask for advice?

GETTING STARTED

Warm Up

1 Many people complain about stress in their lives. These people feel nervous and upset. When someone is under too much stress, we say that this person is "stressed out." What makes people stressed out?

2 Listen to the conversations. Who is stressed out? Circle the name.
  a. Sue / Bob
  b. Judy / Chris
  c. Sandy / Mark

Figure It Out

3 How well do you handle stress? Fill out the questionnaire on page 86 to find out. Circle one or more letters for each question.

Questionnaire

1. **You always carry an expensive, brown briefcase. You are on the bus, and** the **man who is sitting next to you keeps looking at your briefcase. Finally, he says that your briefcase is the one that he lost on the bus last week. You:**
   a. get nervous.
   b. get angry and tell him the briefcase is yours.
   c. don't listen to him and continue reading.
   d. tell him that maybe his briefcase is in the lost and found.

2. **You are alone in an elevator that has stopped between floors. You:**
   a. begin to shout for help.
   b. feel very nervous and frightened.
   c. ring the alarm and calmly wait for help.
   d. read the newspaper you have in your briefcase.

3. **You are going on vacation with your family on Saturday. On Friday morning, an executive who is very important asks you to start work on a new project right away. She says that you can go on vacation next month. You:**
   a. laugh nervously.
   b. feel anxious, but finally agree.
   c. politely refuse and tell why.
   d. suggest that you can start the project after your trip.

4. **You have a friend who wants to borrow some money. He always pays it back, but it takes a long time. Today he needs thirty dollars, but you want to use this money to buy a birthday present for another friend. You:**
   a. get really upset and tell him to find the money some place else.
   b. lend him the money and disappoint your other friend.
   c. explain why you can't lend him the money.
   d. offer to help him learn to use his money more carefully.

5. **You are returning from a trip abroad. You have brought eight Swiss watches with you. The customs officer who is checking your baggage has just told you that the limit is two watches. You:**
   a. begin to get upset.
   b. say that you are very, very sorry.
   c. calmly admit that you have brought in too many watches.
   d. smile and tell him that you didn't know that the limit was two watches.

(4) Count 1 point for every **a** or **b** answer you did *not* circle and 1 point for every **c** or **d** answer you *did* circle. Then find your score in the chart.

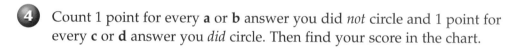

16–20	You handle stress better than most people. You stay calm in situations that make other people very nervous.
11–15	You are a person who sometimes feels stress, but not very often.
6–10	Situations that cause stress are frequent in your life. You should try to relax a little!
0–5	You feel stressed out too often! You should learn how to calm down from people who know how to handle stress.

5 **Vocabulary Check** Match the words and their meanings.

_____ **1.** to handle   **a.** afraid

_____ **2.** frightened   **b.** to control

_____ **3.** anxious   **c.** to make someone feel sad

_____ **4.** to suggest   **d.** nervous

_____ **5.** to disappoint   **e.** the most you can have

_____ **6.** limit   **f.** to say an idea

_____ **7.** to calm down   **g.** to stop being nervous

Talk About It

 6 A reporter for a health magazine is talking to an expert on stress. With a partner, take turns asking and answering questions.

Example: change jobs a lot/never change jobs

Ask for a comparison.

A: Who has more stress—people who change jobs a lot or people who never change jobs?

Give a comparison.

B: People who change jobs have more stress than people who don't.

Ask for an explanation.

A: Why do you think that?

Give an explanation.

B: Because people who change jobs a lot have to make many adjustments in their lives, and that's stressful.

---

a. have money problems/have problems with their children

b. lose their jobs/change work hours every week

c. travel a lot on business/work weekends

d. work for a male boss/work for a female boss

e. give up smoking/go on a diet

GRAMMAR

Adjective Clauses

Adjective clauses define, or give more information about, a noun. They are generally introduced by a relative pronoun (*that, who, whom, which*) and come after the noun they describe.

I have a friend.	*adjective clause* I have a friend **who is stressed out**.
He's listening to a tape.	*adjective clause* He's listening to a tape **which will relax him**.
Many people are stressed out.	*adjective clause* Many people **that I know** are stressed out.

1 Look at the example in the box on page 87:

    a. What does *who* refer to? _____

    b. What does *which* refer to? _____

    c. What does *that* refer to? _____

2 Imagine a stressed-out friend of yours. Finish the sentences.

    a. I have a friend who _____, and who _____.

    b. She works at a place which _____.

    c. She has a car that _____.

We often use adjective clauses to define general words such as *the one, someone, anyone, people, something, anything, everyone*.

In this job, we need **someone** who never gets angry.

Everything that happens at work stresses Leslie out.

---

3 Finish the sentences about your other stressed-out friend, Tom.

    a. Tom doesn't know anyone who _____.

    b. Everything that _____ costs too much.

    c. He doesn't like anything that _____.

    d. He should talk to someone who _____.

Relative Pronouns as Subjects

Relative pronouns can be the subject of the adjective clause. *That* and *which* refer to things. *That* and *who* refer to people.

	Subject	Verb phrase
I read an article	**that**	explains the physical effects of stress.
	which	
I met the doctor	**that**	wrote the article.
	who	

4 Combine each pair of sentences. Use *who* for people and *that* for things.

Example:

I read a book. The book describes how to reduce stress.

I read a book that describes how to reduce stress.

    a. The book is about techniques. The techniques can help you control stress.

    b. The doctor is an expert on stress. The doctor wrote the book.

    c. The book says that running is a technique. This technique can lower stress.

    d. People feel much better. People run three times a week.

    e. Older people often feel depressed. These people live alone.

Relative Pronouns as Objects

A relative pronoun can be the object of the adjective clause. In this case, the pronoun can be left out.

	Object	Subject	Verb		
I read the book	**which**	Dr. Stone	wrote.		Formal
I read the book	**that**	Dr. Stone	wrote.		↓
I read the book	—	Dr. Stone	wrote.		Informal
The man	**whom**	I	met	is an expert on stress.	Formal
The man	**who**	I	met	is an expert on stress.	↓
The man	**that**	I	met	is an expert on stress.	
The man	—	I	met	is an expert on stress.	Informal

5 **Check Your Understanding** Underline the relative pronouns used as subjects. Circle the relative pronouns used as objects. If the pronoun can be left out, put parentheses ( ) around it.

  a. The workers who performed repetitive tasks suffered from stress.
  b. Here are the books on stress that I told you to read.
  c. The child that we saw on the elevator was frightened.
  d. Environmental problems which cause stress include noise and air pollution.
  e. Students who need to get good grades often feel stressed out.

6 Read the paragraph. Write *who* or *which* on the line. If the relative pronoun is not necessary, put it in parentheses ( ).

One thing **(1.)** _____ doctors recommend for people **(2.)** _____ are under a lot of stress is running. Running is a sport **(3.)** _____ anyone can do. It is also a sport **(4.)** _____ doesn't require a lot of special equipment. The only things **(5.)** _____ runners need are running shoes and a place to run. Most people **(6.)** _____ run regularly say that the best place to run is a street or a park. People run outdoors all year round, even in places **(7.)** _____ are cold in the winter. According to experts, people **(8.)** _____ are interested in lowering stress must run for at least twenty to thirty minutes three times a week.

7 **Express Yourself** Look at how adjective clauses are used in definitions. Then, with a partner, complete the chart. Share your sentences with the class.

Example:

A: How would you define a "modem"?

B: It's a device that's used to connect your computer to the Internet.

Item	Verb	Class	Defining Information
A thermometer	is	an instrument	that measures temperature.
A cell phone		a device	
Chocolate	is		
Politicians		people	
A fax machine		a machine	
A stuntman	is		
Idea of your own			

LISTENING and SPEAKING

Listen: Stressful Jobs

1 **Before You Listen** How stressful do you think these jobs are? In column 1, rank them from 1 (highest stress) to 6 (lowest stress).

	1	2		1	2
librarian	___	___	banker	___	___
police officer	___	___	firefighter	___	___
sports star	___	___	actor/actress	___	___

STRATEGY **Identifying Opinions** Listen for expressions such as *personally*, *I think*, *in my opinion*, and *as I see it*. These tell you that the speaker is giving his or her own opinion.

2 Listen to the interview with an expert on stress. In column 2, write his ranking for stress (1 is the highest, 6 is the lowest).

3 Listen to the interview again. What expressions did the speaker use to indicate he was giving his opinion?

4 Compare your rankings with the expert's. Did you rank the jobs differently? Why? Share your ideas with the class.

Pronunciation

> **Contrastive Stress**
>
> In English we use stress and intonation to emphasize or contrast certain information.
>
> **What** did Zoltan buy?   He bought a **car**.   (not a **bike**)
>
> **Did** Zoltan **sell** a car?   No, he **bought** a car.   (not **sold**)
>
> **Who** bought a car?   **Zoltan** bought a car.   (not **Karl**)

5 Work with a partner. Take turns saying the sentences aloud. Is your partner emphasizing the right information?

    a. I never drove my father's new **car**, but I drove his new **motorcycle**.

    b. I never drove my father's **new** car, but I drove his **old** car.

    c. I never drove my **father's** new car, but I drove my **mother's** new car.

    d. I never drove **my** father's new car, but I drove **your** father's new car.

    e. I never **drove** my father's new car, but I **rode** in my father's new car.

    f. I never drove my father's new car, but **you** drove my father's new car.

 6 Listen to the answer and circle the letter of the correct question.

    1. a. Who bought the best computer?
       b. Which computer is best?

    2. a. Which computer did he buy at the mall?
       b. Where did he buy his new computer?

    3. a. Who bought the cheapest computer?
       b. Which computer did Dan buy?

    4. a. How often does Dan use the computer lab?
       b. What time does Dan use the computer lab?

    5. a. Whose computer was the most powerful?
       b. What was Dan's computer like?

Speak Out

STRATEGY **Expressing Preferences** To indicate that you like one person or thing more than another, you use certain expressions. These expressions signal preferences.

I prefer ...	I much prefer ...	Would you rather ... ?
I like ... more than ...	I'd rather ...	I'd rather not ...

7 Work in groups of three. For each word in the box, tell what kinds of things you prefer.

Example:

A: I like movies that have happy endings.

B: Not me! I prefer movies that are frightening.

C: Really? I think scary movies are stressful. I'd rather see movies that teach me something.

READING and WRITING

Read About It

1 **Before You Read**

a. What do you know about chocolate? Where does it come from? What is it made of?

b. The following article about chocolate appears in this unit on stress. What do you think chocolate and stress have to do with each other?

STRATEGY **Understanding Reference** Pronouns are used as substitutes for other words. They can refer to words or phrases that appear earlier or later in the text. By paying attention to pronoun reference, it is easier to understand connections between ideas.

Chocolate: A World Favorite

Chocolate, one of the most popular foods in the world, has a history as rich as its flavor. Chocolate comes from the beans of the cacao tree, a plant that has grown in the Americas for
5   at least 4,000 years. As long ago as the twelfth century, Indian families drank chocolate at marriages and other ceremonies. However, chocolate was not known in Europe until 1528, when the Spanish explorer Hernán Cortés
10 brought it to Spain.

Drinking chocolate soon became popular in Spain and quickly spread to the rest of Europe. Three hundred years later, a scientist in Holland learned how to make chocolate into
15 candy. As the years passed, people in countries such as Belgium, Switzerland, and England began to make many kinds of chocolate candy. Today the making of chocolate is a multibillion dollar industry.

Cacao beans

20   There are many reasons why chocolate is so popular. People like its rich, delicious flavor. Some people think that chocolate is even better when combined with other ingredients, such as fruit and nuts. Also, candy makers can make chocolate into decorative shapes, from flowers and hearts to animals, and even to huge statues that weigh as much as 220 pounds (100 kilos).

25   In addition, eating chocolate has helpful physical effects. The sugar and fat in chocolate give people quick energy. This is why mountain climbers often carry chocolate with them. For this same reason, people like to have a candy bar when they're feeling tired.

    Eating chocolate has mental effects, too. Many people crave chocolate in times
30 of stress or emotional upset. Some psychologists explain that people associate chocolate with the happy times of their childhoods. The taste of chocolate reminds them of the food and comfort they received from their mothers. However, physical scientists have developed another explanation. They say that one
35 ingredient of chocolate, phenylethylamine, seems to lower stress.

    There is no doubt that chocolate, with its unique physical and psychological effects and its unmatched flavor, is one of the world's favorite foods.

2   Answer the questions.

    a. Where did chocolate come from?

    b. Who brought chocolate to Europe?

    c. What effect does chocolate have on the human body?

3   Find the following pronouns in the article and underline the word(s) each one refers to. Check your answers with the class.

a. its (line 2)	**d.** its (line 20)	**g.** they (line 28)
b. that (line 4)	**e.** that (line 23)	**h.** their (line 31)
c. it (line 10)	**f.** them (line 27)	**i.** they (line 32)

4   Use the context to determine the meanings of the words. Write short definitions on a sheet of paper. Work without a dictionary.

a. ceremony (line 7)	**f.** physical (line 25)
b. industry (line 19)	**g.** energy (line 26)
c. flavor (line 21)	**h.** mental (line 29)
d. combined (line 21)	**i.** crave (line 29)
e. ingredients (line 22)	**j.** remind (line 32)

Think About It

5   Do you ever eat when you feel stressed out? What do you eat? Does eating that food make you feel better? Why?

6   The article talks about the good effects of eating chocolate. What are some bad effects of chocolate?

Write: Using Examples

One kind of supporting detail is examples. Examples illustrate your ideas and make your writing easier to understand. Examples can be signaled by expressions like *for example*, *for instance*, *like*, and *such as*.

7 Read the paragraph and answer the questions.

How To Handle STRESS!

When you feel stressed out, there are certain techniques you can use to help you calm down. One good technique is to change scenery. For example, if the stress is coming from work, leave your office and take a short walk. Changing your surroundings can help you forget about the problems at work.

Another good way to reduce stress is to face your problems directly. For instance, if you are having problems with your school work, don't ignore them. Talk to a classmate or, even better, to the teacher. Solving the problems will reduce your stress.

The easiest way to lower stress is physical exercise. Experts say that exercise produces certain stress-reducing chemicals in the brain. Whenever you start to feel tense, do your favorite exercise. Swimming, running, and dancing are especially good for reducing stress.

Since our world can sometimes be stressful, it is important to find ways to handle stress.

a. There are three examples in the paragraph. What are they?

b. How are they signaled?

c. What general statements do they support?

Write About It

8 Write a paragraph on how you handle stress or on how you stay healthy. Describe what you do and tell why these activities help. Include at least one example in your paragraph.

9 **Check Your Writing** Reread your paragraph. Does it say what you want it to say? Use the checklist and make revisions as needed.

- Does the topic sentence state the main idea clearly?
- Are the supporting sentences ordered logically?
- Are there enough details and at least one specific example?

1 Complete the conversation with the correct form of the verbs. Use the simple present, simple past, or present perfect tense.

BILL: Hello, Acme Translation Services? I **(1. have)** _____ a letter that I need translated right away.

ACME: **(2. use, ever)** _____ you _____ our company before?

BILL: No. I **(3. send, always)** _____ my work to Speedy Translations up to now, but I **(4. be,** *neg.***)** _____ satisfied, so now I'm trying you.

ACME: How **(5. find out)** _____ you _____ about our company?

BILL: I **(6. see)** _____ your ad in the paper.

ACME: What language **(7. need)** _____ you _____?

BILL: Urdu. **(8. translate)** _____ you _____ Urdu before?

ACME: Sir, we **(9. hear,** *neg.***)** _____ of that language. I'm sorry.

BILL: What? I can't believe it. What kind of company **(10. be)** _____ this?

2 Complete the passage with the correct form of one of the verbs in the box. Use the simple present, the simple past, or the present perfect tense.

decide	help
describe	receive
find	wish

Are you happy in your present job? **(1.)** _____ you ever _____ that you had a different, more exciting job? If so, subscribe to our monthly newsletter, the *Job Bulletin*. The *Job Bulletin* **(2.)** _____ all the positions available in our area. Last year, over 1,275 happy people **(3.)** _____ the job of their dreams through our newsletter. We **(4.)** _____ letters from satisfied customers every month, thanking us for our help. The *Job Bulletin* **(5.)** _____ people find work for over fifteen years! Let us help you, too.

3 Complete the sentences with an appropriate word or expression from the box.

ever	last month
so far	yet
still	since

a. Have you _____ sat at a cafe and watched the people go by?

b. The company hired six new employees _____.

c. Larry can't go because he hasn't finished his homework _____.

d. My husband has been a couch potato _____ he was a teenager!

e. What? You _____ haven't paid the bills?

f. Do we need film? How many photos have you taken _____?

4 Read each situation and write one sentence giving advice. Use *should*, *shouldn't*, *ought to*, or *had better*.

a. My daughter is always late to work, and I'm afraid she's going to lose her job.

_____

b. Pavel saw Eva cheat on the last math test.

_____

c. Antonio has studied English for six years, but he still cannot speak it well.

_____

d. I don't know why Zack does so badly on tests. He stays up all night to study.

_____

e. The president of the company wants to make his employees happy.

_____

5 Complete each sentence with a relative pronoun. Use *who, whom,* or *which*. If the relative pronoun is not necessary, put it in parentheses ( ).

a. That student over there is the one _____ won the Special Achievement Award.

b. Can you lend me your copy of the novel _____ I lost?

c. My computer is the one invention _____ I couldn't live without!

d. The librarian _____ handles reference books is busy.

e. The child _____ performed that piece plays four other instruments.

Vocabulary Review

Complete the sentences with words from the box.

can't stand	industry
controversial	enthusiasm
had better	lend
stress	salary
handle	

1. Most doctors agree that constant _____ has serious health effects.

2. I really _____ people who don't wait their turn.

3. She is the youngest candidate, but the boss likes her energy and _____.

4. You _____ turn in that report today or you'll get into deep trouble!

5. The boss promised Sarah an increase in _____.

6. I don't think you should _____ Frank that money. He always takes forever to pay back what he owes.

7. Nellie Bly wrote about _____ social topics of her day.

8. The making of chocolate is a multi-billion dollar _____.

YOU'VE GOT TO BE KIDDING!

GETTING STARTED

Warm Up

1 Many people want to be the best in what they do. In sports, for example, runners and swimmers try to break records. Think of some athletes who have broken sports records. What records did they break? What other kinds of records do people try to break?

2 You are going to hear conversations with three people who tried to break records. Circle **yes** if the person broke the record and **no** if the person did not.

   a. yes/no   **b.** yes/no   **c.** yes/no

3 Listen to the conversations again. What record was the person trying to break?

   a. _____

   b. _____

   c. _____

Figure It Out

A.

MOM: Ruby, put that book down!
You've been reading it for hours
now. I need your help
in the kitchen.

5   **RUBY:** But this book is great! Just let me finish
this part and then I'll help you. I'm
reading about a man who has set world
records for eating glass and metal.

MOM: Why do you waste your time on
10   science fiction?

RUBY: It's not science fiction. It's true!
Michel Lotito is a real person from France,
and he has been eating glass and metal
since 1959.

15   **MOM:** You're kidding me!

B.

MOM: How much glass has he eaten?

RUBY: Well, so far, he's eaten six chandeliers.
And remember, he's been eating metal objects
all that time, too.

20   **MOM:** What kind of metal objects?

RUBY: It says here that he has eaten ten bicycles, seven
TV sets, a shopping cart, and ...

MOM: That's incredible! How long did it take him to eat
the shopping cart?

25   **RUBY:** He finished it in four and a half days.

MOM: That's amazing! And he's been doing this for over
thirty years? If he's not careful, he's going to end
up in a coffin. Let me see that book.

RUBY: Here. Look at this part.

30   **MOM:** Gee, he even ate a small airplane! This
is unbelievable!

RUBY: Come on, I'll give you a hand in the kitchen
now. Maybe we should make a glass and
metal salad for dinner tonight. And maybe
we can have the Eiffel Tower for dessert.

4 Answer the questions.

a. How long has Michel Lotito been eating
glass and metal?

b. What unusual objects has he eaten?

c. What are Ruby and her mother going to do?

d. Why do some people do unusual things
such as eating glass and metal and
climbing skyscrapers?

e. What unusual thing would you try?

Michel Lotito

Vocabulary Check Match the words with their definitions.

_____ **1.** set records (lines 7–8)   **a.** not use well

_____ **2.** waste (line 9)   **b.** hard to believe

_____ **3.** objects (line 18)   **c.** help

_____ **4.** incredible (line 23)   **d.** things

_____ **5.** give a hand (line 32)   **e.** be the best

Talk About It

6 Each of the guests on today's *That's Amazing!* show has set a world record. Work with a partner. Take turns being the TV show host and the guest. Ask and answer questions using the cues.

Example: Jose Montero's record:
         hit songs written in one year

Ask about number of actions until present.

A: Jose, you've just set the world record for songwriting. How many hits have you written so far this year?

Tell number of actions until present.

B: I've written seven so far this year.

Ask about length of time.

A: How long have you been writing songs?

Tell length of time.

B: I've been composing songs for ten years now … basically since I moved to Hollywood.

a. Gary DiAngelo's record: countries visited in one year

b. Judy Grant's record: film awards won in lifetime

c. Keiko Mayahara's record: sports medals received in lifetime

GRAMMAR

The Present Perfect Progressive Tense: Unfinished Past Actions

The present perfect progressive (*have/has* + *been* + verb–*ing*) is used to talk about unfinished past actions or actions that began in the past, are happening now, and will probably continue into the future.

> **A:** How long **have** you **been singing** opera now?
>
> **B:** Well, I**'ve been working** at the Opera Cafe for a year now.
>
> **A:** **Have** you **liked** your job as a singing waitress?
>
> **B:** Oh yes, I**'ve broken** 100 glasses! I'm the high note of the evening.

1 Write an appropriate verb in the present perfect progressive tense.

1. **A:** Did Michel Lotito really eat six chandeliers?

   B: Why, yes. He _____ glass since 1959.

2. **A:** I understand Natalia has won several swimming medals.

   B: That's right. She _____ medals ever since she was a child.

3. **A:** I hear Lola and Manuel won the prize for the best dancers.

   B: Yes, they _____ in contests since they met each other in 1998.

4. **A:** Is it true that Charles got the award for the person who has traveled the most?

   B: Yes, it is. He _____ for more than forty years now.

5. **A:** I hear you have a huge rock collection.

   B: Yes, I _____ rocks for five years now.

The Present Perfect vs. the Present Perfect Progressive

We use the present perfect tense to talk about actions completed at an indefinite time in the past, but which still have importance in the present.

> He**'s read** the book, so he knows the ending. *(the action is complete)*
>
> He**'s been reading** the book, but he hasn't finished yet. *(the action is incomplete)*

The present perfect tense is often used to tell how many times someone has done an action. The present perfect progressive tense often stresses how long someone has been doing an action.

> He's read the book **five times**.
>
> He's been reading the book **for over a month**.

 2 **Check Your Understanding** Match the sentences with their meanings. Write the letter on the line.

_____ **1.** I've collected stamps for years. I'm starting to get bored with them.

_____ **2.** I've been collecting stamps for years. I'm going to look for more when I go on vacation.

_____ **3.** I collected stamps when I was young.

a. I collected stamps, but I stopped several years ago.

b. I collected stamps in the past, but I may stop soon.

c. I began collecting stamps a while ago, and I am still an active stamp collector.

_____ **4.** She's driven race cars since she was a teenager, but now she wants to learn to fly a plane.

_____ **5.** She's been driving race cars for two years.

_____ **6.** She drove a race car three years ago.

a. She drives a race car now, and she will probably drive it in the future.

b. She doesn't drive a race car now, but she did in the past.

c. She began driving race cars years ago, but she may stop soon.

3 Complete the sentences with a form of the present perfect or the present perfect progressive. Some verbs may be negative.

a. Paul Miller of California **(grow)** _____ his mustache for eleven years now. So far, it **(reach)** _____ a length of more than 6 feet (1.8 meters).

b. Sal Piro of New York City **(see)** _____ the film *The Rocky Horror Picture Show* more than 870 times. Movie theaters **(show)** _____ that film for over eleven years now.

c. Georgia Sebrantke of West Germany **(cut)** _____ her hair since she was born. It's now 10 feet long and still growing.

d. Jan Leighton of the United States **(play)** _____ more than 3,350 different roles so far in his career as an actor.

e. McDonald's, the world's largest chain of hamburger restaurants, **(serve)** _____ hamburgers since 1955. McDonald's **(sell)** _____ more than 90 billion hamburgers.

4 **Express Yourself** Ask a partner about his or her activities.

Example: have any hobbies

A: Do you have any hobbies?

B: Yes, I collect stamps.

A: How long have you been collecting stamps?

B: Since I was ten years old.

a. play a musical instrument
b. exercise regularly
c. own a bike or car
d. look up information on the Internet
e. belong to any clubs or teams
f. idea of your own

5 Work in groups of three. Report your partner's current activities to the group.

Listen: The Talk Show Guest

1 **Before You Listen**

Do UFOs (**u**nidentified **f**lying **o**bjects) exist?
Some people say they have actually seen them.
Do you believe in UFOs? Why or why not?

 Listening to Confirm Predictions You can
often predict in a general way what a talk will be
about. As you listen, focus on information that tells
you if your guesses are correct. Listen to confirm
your predictions.

2 You're watching TV and the announcer says, "Next on *That's Amazing!*,
an interview with a man who says he's seen a UFO and met beings
from another planet." With a partner, predict what probably happened
to the man.

 3 Listen and compare your ideas with the real story.

 4 Now listen to the interview again and answer the questions.

   a. How long has Mr. Quintero been a farmer?

   b. Where did the space people take Mr. Quintero?

   c. What problems has he been having recently?

Pronunciation

Unstressed *h* Words

Unstressed function words beginning with *h* (*him, her, his, have,* etc.) usually drop the
initial /**h**/ sound. The word is then linked to the previous word.

This is **his** medal, not **her** medal. (stressed, no reductions)

Ruby read ~~h~~is book, and so did ~~h~~er Mom. (unstressed, *h* is dropped)
    (read'is)   (did'er)

How long ~~h~~ave you been reading this?
    (long've)

---

 5 Work with a partner. Predict how to say the words. Draw a line
through the letter *h* when you think it's not pronounced. Then draw
a line linking the function word to the previous word.

   A: So Hilary, how long have you and Henry been living in Prague?

   B: I just got here, but Henry's been here for half a year.

   A: How does he like it here? Has Prague been good to him?

   B: He says he's the happiest he's ever been.

A: Wow! That's amazing! He must really like his job.

B: He does, and his boss, and his office, and his house.

A: And I'm sure he adores his wife, Hilary.

B: I hope so. Anyway, I'm really happy for him.

 6 Now listen to the dialogue and check your predictions.

7 Practice reading the dialogue, focusing on linking the words.

Speak Out

 Expressing Surprise or Disbelief When you hear information that is surprising or hard to believe, you can use these expressions.

Wow!	That's hard to believe.	Oh, come on!
That's amazing!	You can't be serious.	I can't believe it.
You're kidding me!	Are you really sure that …	No way!

8 Work in groups of three. Each student reads one of the texts below. Then close your books and take turns telling the stories to each other. As a group, decide which of the stories is false. (Only one is false.) Use the language for showing surprise to react to your partners' stories.

A. Carolyn James has been painting bright, happy pictures of the English countryside since 1980. She has sold many of her paintings for thousands of dollars. She begins by sitting in a pretty place and drawing it. Later, she finishes her paintings at home. James's paintings are unusual not only because they are beautiful—they are also unusual because she is totally blind.

B. Bill Harding is a performer from Chicago, Illinois, who has some very unique clothes. They are made of real grass that is still alive and growing. Harding has developed a special technique to grow grass between pieces of cloth. He has been looking for a company to sell his grass pants, shirts, dresses, and shoes, but so far no one has been interested.

C. Frank Faruggio is a chemist from Atlanta, Georgia, the home of Coca-Cola. He has spent eleven years on an unusual project. He has been working on the world's first soft-drink bottle you can eat. After people drink the soft drink, they can eat the bottle. He says that his bottles will be ready for supermarkets by 2005.

Read About It

1 Before You Read

   a. Reference books, such as a telephone book or thesaurus, are useful tools for finding information. List as many reference books as you can.

   b. One kind of reference book is a book of records. What information can you find in this sort of book?

STRATEGY ▶ **Distinguishing Fact and Opinion** When you read, it is important to tell the difference between facts and opinions. Facts are statements that are known to be true. Opinions are expressions of a writer's ideas, beliefs, or emotions.

A Record-Breaking Book

   People have always been interested in learning about world records. They want to know the biggest, smallest, fastest, slowest, longest, shortest, oldest,
5 and youngest. However, until 1955 there was no single reference book that contained comparative information on world records. The first book of this kind was the *Guinness Book*
10 *of World Records.*

   The idea for this book came from Hugh Beaver, who was an executive of Arthur Guinness Son and Co., Ltd. One day, after seeing some birds flying, he
15 told his friends that he thought that those birds were probably the fastest birds in Britain. Several of his friends disagreed with him. However, when they tried to settle the argument by looking in
20 various reference books, they found out that none contained the information that they were looking for. As a result, Beaver decided that his company ought to put out a book that would present all sorts of superlatives and world records.

Beaver began to look for authors. Soon he heard of Norris
25 and Ross McWhirter, who ran a small fact and figure agency in
London. They found and checked facts for people and so had
gathered a large collection of information from newspapers,
magazines, reference books, and other sources. Beaver
interviewed the two brothers in order to test their knowledge
30 of records and unusual facts. He found their knowledge
amazing and hired them. On August 27, 1955, the *Guinness
Book of Superlatives* went on sale in bookstores. In four
months it became a best seller. Later, the name of the book
was changed to the *Guinness Book of World Records.*

35 The *Guinness Book of World Records* has fascinated
people ever since it came out. The public continues to buy new versions of the book
every year. In fact, since 1988, the book has had average sales of 60 million copies a
year in 25 languages. This number equals 168 stacks of books each as tall as Mount
Everest. Even today, this book continues to break its own record as the fastest selling
40 book in the world!

2 Read the statements. Write **T** (true) or **F** (false).

a. ____ Beaver and his friend found that the birds were in fact the
fastest birds in Britain.

b. ____ Beaver hired Norris and Ross McWhirter to write a book.

c. ____ At first, the *Guinness Book of Superlatives* was not popular.

3 Decide if each statement is a fact **(F)** or opinion **(O)**. Write **F** or **O**.

____ **a.** People have always been interested in world records.

____ **b.** Hugh Beaver was an executive of Arthur Guinness,
Son and Co., Ltd.

____ **c.** Beaver thought Norris and Ross McWhirter's knowledge
was amazing.

____ **d.** On August 27, 1955, the *Guinness Book of Superlatives*
went on sale.

____ **e.** The *Guinness Book of World Records* is a fascinating book.

4 Use the context to guess the meanings of the
words. Write synonyms or definitions on a
sheet of paper. Work without a dictionary.

a. single (line 6)

b. contained (lines 7 and 21)

c. settle (line 19)

d. put out (line 22)

e. sources (line 28)

f. knowledge (line 29)

g. best seller (line 33)

h. version (line 36)

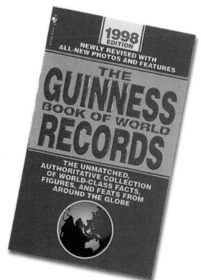

Think About It

5 Which is more useful—studying hard and memorizing many facts, or knowing where to look to get facts when you need them? Why?

6 In addition to reference books, today many people use the Internet to get information. Do you think you can trust information found on the Internet? How can you tell if it is accurate?

Write: Using Transitions

To connect our ideas in writing, we use linking words, called transitions. These words tell readers what to expect next in a paragraph. Some transitions show relationships such as time and rank. Others signal additional information (*and, also, in addition*) or effect/result (*so, therefore, for this reason*).

7 Combine the sentences to form a paragraph. Use the linking words in the box. Write the paragraph on a sheet of paper.

after that	in addition
as a result	soon
finally	therefore
for example	

    a. I have been breaking records for walking on my hands for a long time.
    b. I set a record in 1988 when I walked one mile.
    c. I tried to walk farther, but my arms were not strong enough.
    d. I began a very difficult training program.
    e. I began lifting weights.
    f. I tried to walk a little farther on my hands every day.
    g. I began to increase my distances.
    h. I broke a record by walking on my hands from New York to Montreal.

Write About It

8 Imagine that you have just set a world record. Pick a record and tell how you set it. Make sure that your paragraph has a clear topic sentence, several supporting sentences, and a concluding sentence. Use transition words in your paragraph.

9 Exchange papers with another student. Make suggestions to your partner. If there are places where you need more information, write a question to the writer in the margin.

10 **Check Your Writing** When you get your paper back, use the questions below and make revisions as needed.

- Is the main idea developed with enough supporting ideas and details?
- Are transition words used to show relationships between ideas?
- Are verb tenses used correctly?

GETTING STARTED

Warm Up

1 When someone gets rich quickly, we say that the person has gone "from rags to riches." Do you know of anyone who has gone from rags to riches? (A businessperson? A movie star? A musician?) How has the person's life changed?

2 Listen to the conversations. How did the people get rich? Write the number of the conversation in the box. There is one extra picture.

3 "Money can't buy happiness" is an old saying. Do you agree? What are the advantages and disadvantages of being rich? Brainstorm a list.

Figure It Out

A few numbers on a lottery ticket have completely changed the lives of George and Mary Buck and their three children. Susan Johnson of WXYZ-TV is interviewing them.

A.   **SUSAN:**   Well, Mr. and Mrs. Buck, it's been six months since that lucky day! How are you getting used to your new life of luxury?

              GEORGE: It's been great! But we've had to make a lot of adjustments.

	SUSAN:	Really? What kinds of adjustments?
5	GEORGE:	Well, I used to get up early and work long hours. I never used to spend much time with the children because I went to bed right after dinner. I was always exhausted by the end of the day.
10	MARY:	And I was always worrying about money. There never seemed to be enough to pay all the bills. We never went to fancy restaurants or took nice vacations.
15	GEORGE:	Now our lives are completely different. We sleep late, have our meals by the pool, and take long trips. I can even afford to buy Mary gold jewelry!

B.	SUSAN:	What kinds of things have you bought?
20	GEORGE:	Well, our house, of course. Plus, we bought each of our children a new car. They used to take the bus to school. Now they drive!

	SUSAN:	Have you gotten used to your new house?
25	MARY:	Well, it's much larger than our old one. It's got a huge pool, a bowling alley, a private movie theater, and all the latest appliances.
	GEORGE:	And of course, we don't have to cook or clean anymore because we have a chef and a maid.

C.	SUSAN:	Has your social life changed much?
30	GEORGE:	It sure has! I used to go bowling with my friends after work. Now I can invite them to bowl here.
	MARY:	And I never used to go to the movies. It was too expensive. But now I can invite all of my friends to watch the latest movies right here at home.
35	SUSAN:	So, is it true that money can buy happiness?
	MARY:	Not really. We still have a few worries, but being rich has made some things a lot easier!

4 Answer the questions.

a. How did the Buck family get rich?

b. What did they use to do before they got rich?

c. Why didn't Mary Buck use to go to the movies?

d. Imagine you win the lottery. How will your life be different? What will you do? Name five things.

e. There is a saying, "Love of money is the root of all evil." Do you agree? Why or why not?

 5 **Vocabulary Check** Write a synonym or short definition for each of the following words. Work without a dictionary.

a. luxury (line 2)   d. bills (line 12)   g. chef (line 28)

b. adjustments (line 3) e. afford (line 18)   h. maid (line 28)

c. exhausted (line 7)   f. appliances (line 26)   i. the latest (line 33)

Talk About It

 6 You are interviewing the Buck children about what they used to do before they got rich and what they do now. With a partner, take turns asking and answering questions about the cues below. The first is done for you.

Ask about past routine.

A: Did you use to eat out in expensive restaurants?

Describe past routine.

B: Oh no, we never used to eat out in fancy restaurants. We always used to eat at home.

Current Activities	Past Activities
a. eat out in expensive restaurants	always eat at home
b. play computer games	not have a computer
c. watch movies in a private theater	not go to the movies
d. go to live concerts	listen to old tapes
e. drive a car to school	take the bus to school
f. ask the chef to cook something	prepare our own meals
g. wear new designer clothes	wear the same clothes for a long time

GRAMMAR

Habitual Actions in the Past: *Used to* + Verb

When we talk about actions that happened regularly in the past, we can use the simple past tense with an adverb of frequency or an expression of frequency.

George and Mary **frequently had** hot dogs in their backyard when they lived in their old house. They **never ate** gourmet foods.

We can also use the expression *used to* + verb to talk about past habits or past routines. *Used to* is pronounced /yuwstə/.

> **A:** In those days, Mary and George **used to serve** their guests hamburgers and hot dogs. They **didn't use to have** a fancy chef.
>
> **B:** **Did** they **use to eat** off of paper plates then?
>
> **A:** Of course. They didn't have a dishwasher in those days.

1 Look at the sentences in the box above. Circle the answer.

   a. In affirmative sentences we use   use to   used to.

   b. In negative sentences we use   use to   used to.

   c. In questions we use   use to   used to.

2 Fill in the blanks with the correct form of *used to*.

MARY: George, I'm bored. I think I **(1. be)** _____ happier before we won the lottery.

GEORGE: You're kidding me! Now we have everything that money can buy.

MARY: I know, but I miss my old friends. Jane and I always **(2. do)** _____ our laundry at the Laundromat every week. And Cathy and I **(3. go)** _____ grocery shopping together. We **(4. try)** _____ to plan inexpensive meals. Now the chef and the maid do everything.

GEORGE: You **(5. think, *neg.*)** _____ our life was so good.

MARY: I know, but I do now. We **(6. be)** _____ happy just being together. Remember?

GEORGE: Of course I remember. But why **(7. you, worry)** _____ about money all the time? And why **(8. you, complain)** _____ that you had to work too hard? Now we never have to worry about money again.

MARY: True. But money isn't everything.

3 David started his first year at college two months ago and is living in an apartment with two roommates. His life has really changed. Complete the chart with what you imagine used to happen at home.

Home	College
David's mother used to make all the meals.	David cooks for himself.
	He gets up at 10:30 a.m.
	He does his laundry every other week.
	He pays bills.
	He comes home when he wants.
	He studies in the library.

4 With a partner, ask and answer questions about what David used to do.

Example:

A: Did David use to cook for himself?

B: No, he never used to cook. His mother used to make all the meals. Now, he cooks for himself, but he only knows how to microwave food.

Get used to and Be used to

When we are in the process of adjusting to changes, we use the expression *get used to* + verb–*ing*. When we have finished adjusting, we use the expression *be used to* + verb–*ing*.

A: How have you adjusted to living in Barcelona?

B: At first, it was difficult, but now I love it. And I**'m** even **getting used to eating** lunch at 2 p.m. and dinner at 9 p.m.

A: **Are** you **used to speaking** Catalan yet?

B: Oh, yes. I have no problems with Catalan.

Get used to and *be used to* can also be followed by a noun phrase or pronoun.

A: When you moved to Barcelona, was it hard to **get used to Catalan**?

B: No, actually, I **got used to it** pretty fast—thanks to Catalan TV.

---

 5 **Check Your Understanding**

Which form means "you have finally adjusted to changes"?

   a. *get used to* + verb–*ing*   **b.** *be used to* + verb–*ing*

Which form means "you are still adjusting to changes"?

   a. *get used to* + verb–*ing*   **b.** *be used to* to + verb–*ing*

6 Read about Kyung-mi. Write a correct form of *be used to* or *get used to* on the line. Discuss your answers with a partner.

   a. Kyung-mi has just moved from a village in Korea to New York City. After a year, it all seems a little less strange to her. Kyung-mi _____ to New York, slowly but surely.

   b. Kyung-mi studied English in Korea for many years. After a year of living and studying in New York City, she is no longer afraid to speak English. Finally, Kyung-mi _____ speaking English.

   c. At first, Kyung-mi was surprised at all the different people in New York City. On the subway, she used to stare at young people who wore colorful clothes and had crazy hairdos. Now she hardly notices them. Kyung-mi _____ seeing a lot of different kinds of people.

7 Use the correct form of *used to*, *get used to*, or *be used to* with the verbs in parentheses. You may need to use the negative.

GLORIA VANDERBILT

Gloria Vanderbilt is from one of the richest families in New York. She's always been rich, but she hasn't always been happy. In fact, Vanderbilt **(1. be)** _____ very unhappy. As a child, she lived with an aunt, but her aunt **(2. spend)** _____ much time with her. Vanderbilt never had any real friends because she didn't go to school. Private teachers **(3. come)** _____ to her house to teach her.

At age seventeen, Vanderbilt went to Hollywood and her life changed. She quickly **(4. dance)** _____ at famous clubs. She even **(5. date)** _____ movie stars. But she was still not happy. She thought people liked her only for her money.

Now Vanderbilt is a very successful clothing designer. Millions of people wear her jeans. Her success changed her social life, too. Finally, she made friends who like her for herself. She **(6. be)** _____ famous and popular. Gloria Vanderbilt is happy at last.

8 **Check Your Understanding** In which situations are you likely to use *used to* + verb?

☐ Talking about when you were a child
☐ Describing what your life was like before you bought a car
☐ Explaining to a friend how to use a cellular phone
☐ Deciding whether to buy a laptop or a desktop computer
☐ Interviewing someone who has just moved to a new country about their past

Compare your answers with a partner's.

9 **Express Yourself** With a partner, pick one of the situations you checked above. Imagine yourselves in the situation and write a dialogue.

Listen: What Went Wrong?

1 **Before You Listen** Many travelers look for small villages and clean beaches that are relatively unknown and free of tourists. Eventually, other tourists find these places. What happens when these places become popular?

STRATEGY **Listening for Tone of Voice** When you listen, pay attention to the speaker's tone of voice. The tone tells you how he or she is feeling or what he or she really means.

2 Listen to an interview with people from a small village that suddenly became very popular. Circle the correct answer.

    a. The interviewer's tone is   impatient   neutral   humorous.

    b. The villager's tone is   sad   irritated   hesitant.

    c. The young villager's tone is   enthusiastic   sarcastic   angry.

3 Listen again. Write **T** (true) or **F** (false) on the line. Correct any false statement.

    ——— **a.** Most of the people used to be farmers or fishermen.

    ——— **b.** The young people never used to go out dancing in clubs.

    ——— **c.** Many local couples have gotten married in the last five years.

    ——— **d.** There are 1,300 hotel beds for tourists.

    ——— **e.** The people are used to the tourists' customs.

4 With a partner, discuss how the villagers solved their problems. Then look on page 116 to check your answer.

Pronunciation

> **Unstressed *to***
>
> Like other function words, *to* is usually unstressed. The vowel sound **/uw/** is reduced to /ə/, and sometimes the /t/ is dropped. *To* is also linked to the word before it.
>
> | I **used to** get up early. | /yustə/ | She's **going to** get up early. | /gənə/ |
> |---|---|---|---|
> | You **ought to** get up earlier. | /ɔtə/ | I've **got to** get up early. | /gɔtə/ |
> | I **want to** get up early. | /wanə/ | I **have to** get up early. | /hæftə/ |

5 Read the conversation. Predict how to pronounce *to*. Then listen to the conversation. Draw a line through *to* if it is reduced.

    A: What are you going to do tonight?

    B: I'm going to go to the movies. Do you want to come along?

    A: I can't. I've got to study. Don't you have to study, too?

    B: Yes, but I'm going to the movies first. Don't worry. I'm used to studying late.

Check your answers with a partner. Then practice reading the dialogue, focusing on the correct pronunciation of *to*.

Speak Out

STRATEGY **Introducing a New Topic and Returning to a Topic** When you want to change the subject of a conversation or return to the previous topic, you can use certain words and expressions.

Introducing a New Topic	Returning to a Topic
That reminds me …	But to get back to …
Speaking of …	As I was saying …

 Work in groups of three. Imagine a profession that you used to have. Discuss your past experiences with the group.

Example:

A: I used to be a clown. I really liked my job. I was a clown for ten years! I used to work in all the most famous circuses.

B: That reminds me of when I went to the circus to paint pictures of the performers. You see, I used to be a painter.

C: Really? I love art. I used to live right by the Modern Art Museum.

A: Well, as I was saying, I used to work in really big circuses …

READING and WRITING

Read About It

 Before You Read Describe the home of your dreams. Is it a huge house? A luxury apartment? Is it in the country or the city? What special features does it have?

STRATEGY **Summarizing** One way to help you understand and remember a reading is to summarize the most important ideas in a few simple words. When you summarize, include the main idea of each paragraph and use your own words.

 Read the following article and decide which ideas you would include in a summary of the reading.

San Simeon—One Man's Dream

San Simeon, a fantastic estate on the central California coast, was the brainchild of William Randolph Hearst. Hearst, a newspaper and magazine publisher, was one of the richest men of the early twentieth century. His dream was to use his wealth to build a huge castle filled with the world's most beautiful art and architecture.

5　　　Hearst began building his castle in 1920.
He named it San Simeon, but he used to refer
to it and the surrounding hillside as "the
ranch," a simple place for his family and
friends to gather. Eventually, in addition to
10　the castle, he built three villas for guests and
a zoo. The estate covered more than 200,000
acres, with a private beach over 50 miles long.

San Simeon

　　　Hearst designed many of San Simeon's
rooms himself, but he chose the architect Julia Morgan to design the house. Hearst and
15　Morgan worked on the house for many years. They often changed their plans in order
to make the house better. At times, they even tore down what they had built because
Hearst had changed his mind. When Morgan told him that the view from his bedroom
windows would not be very good, he added a second floor so his bedroom would be
higher and have a better view. After a guest mentioned that the swimming pool was
20　too small, Hearst began building the largest heated outdoor pool in the world.

　　　Hearst used the finest wood and stone to build his castle. In addition, he sent
people all over the world to find beautiful objects to fill its rooms. They brought back
Greek statues, Spanish wood ceilings and furniture, entire rooms from European
castles, and even complete buildings to use as building materials. Hearst's art
25　collection, the largest ever owned by one man, contained treasures from every part of
the world and was worth millions of dollars. However, Hearst never felt satisfied with
his castle. He continued working on it, planning more rooms and buildings, until his
death in 1937.

　　　Many people wonder if San Simeon made Hearst happy.
30　Perhaps not. When people entered the house after he died,
they found that many of the treasures were still in their
boxes. Hearst had never looked at or enjoyed some of his
most beautiful possessions. Also, the constant changes that
he made may show that, for him, the house was never
35　perfect or complete.

　　　San Simeon has been a public museum since 1958.
Since then, hundreds of thousands of people have seen for
themselves one of the world's largest and most beautiful
examples of the power of money.

William Randolph Hearst

 Answer the questions.

    a. What was Hearst's dream?
    b. Who designed San Simeon?
    c. Where did Hearst buy the objects he put in his castle?

 Using the context, write a synonym or definition of each word.

    a. brainchild (line 1)　　　　　　**e.** tore down (line 16)
    b. wealth (line 3)　　　　　　　　**f.** changed his mind (line 17)
    c. surrounding (line 7)　　　　　　**g.** satisfied with (line 26)
    d. eventually (line 9)　　　　　　　**h.** treasures (line 31)

5 Summarize each paragraph of the article on San Simeon.

Example: Paragraph 1

San Simeon was built by William Hearst, one of the wealthiest men of the twentieth century. It is a large house full of beautiful art and architecture.

Think About It

6 What are some examples of interesting architecture in your country? Who built these buildings? What are they used for?

7 Ancient treasures of great beauty, such as the Aztec carvings in Mexico or the fragments of temples and statues in Greece, form part of the world's cultural heritage. Should people have the right to buy these treasures for themselves or should they belong exclusively to their country of origin?

Write: Summarizing

A summary presents the most important ideas of a reading in a shortened form. It should include the main ideas and main supporting points, but not the details. The first sentence of a summary usually mentions the title and the main idea of the text.

Write About It

8 Write a summary of the reading in Unit 9, "Chocolate: A World Favorite." You can start like this:

The article "Chocolate: A World Favorite" explains the popularity of chocolate throughout the world.

 9 **Check Your Writing** Exchange papers with a partner. Use the questions below to give your partner feedback. Then, revise your paper as necessary.

- Does the first sentence name the article and give the main idea?
- Does the summary include only the main ideas and the main supporting points, not details?
- Is the summary written in the writer's words?

> Answer to Exercise 4 on p. 113: The people built another village on a hillside, not far from the old village. The people work in the old village, but go home to their new village.

GETTING STARTED

Warm Up

1 Some TV game shows give people a chance to win big prizes. When someone wins a big prize, such as a new house or a car, we say that he or she has "hit the jackpot." What kind of game shows have you seen on TV? Do you like game shows? Why or why not?

2 You are going to listen to parts of two game shows. What do you think the name of each show is? Write the number on the line.

_____ *Name the Song!*   _____ *What's My Occupation?*
_____ *The $44,000 Question*   _____ *Guess the Price!*

Figure It Out

Jackpot Shop is a popular TV game show that takes place in a shopping mall. Contestants try to win fabulous prizes, such as computers, TVs, cars, appliances, and jewelry.

A.   BETTY: Hello, and welcome to the show! I'm your hostess, Betty DiGato. This week our contestants are Maria Duran and Peter Flanigan. [*applause*] Maria and Peter, I hope you aren't too nervous.

	PETER:	Not at all, Betty, this is my third week on the show, so I'm
5		getting used to it.
	MARIA:	I'm thrilled to be here, but yes, I'm a bit nervous. I've never been on TV before!
	BETTY:	Before we begin, I want to make sure you understand the rules. First, you pick out one of our fabulous prizes from any
10		of the shops in the mall. Then you have to answer a question. If the prize is inexpensive, the question will be easy. However, if you choose a more expensive prize, such as a digital TV, the question will be harder. If you answer correctly, you win the prize. Do you have any questions?
15	**MARIA:**	If I make a mistake, do I get the prize?
	BETTY:	No, if you make a mistake, you won't win anything. And you'll have to give back the most expensive prize you've won.
B.	**BETTY:**	Remember, the player who has the most prizes at the end of the game gets to answer the jackpot question! And if the
20		player answers correctly, he or she hits the jackpot. The jackpot is ten minutes of free shopping in the mall. If the player answers the jackpot question incorrectly, he or she still gets to come back and play again next week.
	MARIA:	What if I don't answer any questions correctly?
25	**BETTY:**	You'll still get a copy of my autobiography, *Famous in Fifteen Minutes.* Everybody's a winner on *Jackpot Shop*!

3 Answer the questions.

a. How do players win prizes on *Jackpot Shop?*
b. What happens if a player answers a question incorrectly?
c. What is the jackpot?
d. Would you like to participate in a game show? Why or why not?
e. What is more important for a game-show contestant, intelligence or luck? Why?
f. Do you consider yourself a lucky person? Why or why not?

4 **Vocabulary Check** Write definitions for the following words.

a. hostess (line 1)
b. contestants (line 2)
c. thrilled (line 6)
d. rules (line 9)
e. pick out (line 9)
f. fabulous (line 9)
g. hit the jackpot (line 20)
h. copy (line 25)
i. autobiography (line 25)
j. winner (line 26)

Talk About It

5 You are checking with Betty DiGato about the rules of *Jackpot Shop*. Work with a partner. Use the cues and take turns asking questions.

Example: answer question correctly

Ask a question about a condition.

A: What happens if I answer the question correctly?

State the possible result of the condition.

B: If you answer the question correctly, you'll win the prize.

a. pick out cheap prize
b. answer question incorrectly
c. my opponent gets answer correct
d. choose expensive prize

e. not get any questions right
f. answer jackpot question correctly
g. not give back prizes
h. make mistake with jackpot question

GRAMMAR

The First Conditional: Possible Results

In conditional sentences, the *if* clause is the condition, and the main clause is the result of that condition. First conditional sentences show results that are possible in the present or future.

Condition	Result
If + present simple	present simple
If the player **answers** right,	he **gets** the prize.
If + present simple	will + verb
If we **win** today,	we **will fly** to Rio.
If we **don't win**,	we'**ll stay** home.

The *if* clause can come before or after the main clause.

A: **If we go to Brazil,** we'll stay in Rio.

B: No, I won't go to Brazil **if we don't go up the Amazon.**

1 Complete the conversation with the simple present or future tense of the verbs.

THELMA: If we **(1. win)** _____ a trip, where
(2. we, go) _____?

EARL: We **(3. go)** _____ to Brazil if we
(4. win) _____, right?

THELMA: Right, and if we **(5. go)** _____ to Brazil,
we **(6. take)** _____ a trip up the Amazon.

EARL: No, Thelma. If we **(7. travel)** _____ to Brazil, we **(8. go,** *neg.***)** _____ up the Amazon. We **(9. visit)** _____ Rio and **(10. relax)** _____ on the beach. And we **(11. visit)** _____ Salvador de Bahia. I've always wanted to go there.

THELMA: Well, I've always wanted to take a boat up the Amazon. If you **(12. go,** *neg.***)** _____ up the Amazon with me, I **(13. go,** *neg.***)** _____ to Salvador de Bahia with you.

EARL: OK. But what **(14. we, do)** _____ if we **(15. win,** *neg.***)** _____?

2 You are going to study abroad next year. What will you do if these things happen to you? Write your responses on a sheet of paper.

Example: What if you can't understand the language?

If I can't understand the language, I'll ask people
to repeat.

  a. What if you lose your traveler's checks?
  b. What if you don't get along with your host family?
  c. What if you don't like the food?
  d. What if your parents come to visit?
  e. What if you run out of money?
  f. What if you lose your passport?
  g. What if you get sick?
  h. What if you fall in love?
  i. Idea of your own.

3 Work with a partner. Interview him or her to see if your solutions are the same. Decide which solution is better.

Example:

A: What'll you do if you can't understand the language?

B: No problem. I'll hire a translator.

A: What'll you do if you can't find a translator?

B: In that case, I'll use gestures.

Conditionals with *Unless*

Unless means *if not*. We use *unless* with negative conditions to express requirements or give a strong warning.

Required Condition	Result
If Earl **does not win**,	he **won't go** to Bahia.
Unless Earl **wins**,	he **won't go** to Bahia.
Unless you **go** up the Amazon,	I **won't go** to Bahia.

4 Complete the dialogue with *if* or *unless*.

EARL: I won't go to Brazil **(1.)** _____ we don't stay for at least two weeks. There's no point in going **(2.)** _____ we can enjoy it.

THELMA: Well, I won't go **(3.)** _____ we stay a month. Brazil's the fifth largest country in the world and there's so much to see.

EARL: We won't be able to see the Iguaca Falls **(4.)** _____ we have more time.

THELMA: And **(5.)** _____ we don't see those falls, I'm not going!

5 You are confirming plans with a friend. With a partner, make dialogues using the cues.

Example:

A: You'll go camping with us this weekend, won't you?

B: Of course I will, unless it rains.

a. go camping this weekend
b. get tickets for the new Spielberg movie tomorrow
c. go sightseeing with me after your job interview
d. begin dance lessons next fall
e. sail up the Amazon next summer
f. join the gym in January
g. idea of your own

More on First Conditionals

We can use *should, ought to, can,* and imperatives in first conditionals.

> If you go to Mexico, you **ought to go** to the Yucatan.
>
> If you go to the Yucatan, you **shouldn't miss** the Mayan ruins at Chichen Itza.
>
> If you get tired of the ruins, **drive** to the beach.

6 Mary Lee is going to start college soon. Her father is afraid that everything will go wrong, but Mrs. Lee is sure everything will be OK. Work with a partner. Make dialogues using the cues.

Example: not like her roommate

MR. LEE: What will happen if she doesn't like her roommate?

MRS. LEE: If she doesn't like her roommate, she can move to another apartment.

a. need money
b. get sick
c. forget to call us
d. not get good grades
e. miss home
f. not learn to cook
g. get stressed out
h. need a car
i. want to drop out
j. idea of your own

☑ **7** **Check Your Understanding** In which situations are you likely to use the first conditional? Check your answers with a partner's.

- ☐ Talking about your experiences with dating
- ☐ Warning someone about playing the lottery
- ☐ Describing how the sun affects planets
- ☐ Telling about a frightening experience that you had
- ☐ Explaining the rules of a sport to someone

8 **Express Yourself** With your partner, choose one of the situations you checked above. Imagine yourselves in the situation and write a dialogue using the first conditional.

LISTENING and SPEAKING

Listen: *Jackpot Shop!*

1 **Before You Listen** On *Jackpot Shop*, contestants answer questions to win prizes. In the game shows you know about, what do contestants have to do to win prizes?

STRATEGY **Understanding Numbers** Facts and statistics often include numbers. When you listen to take notes or to answer questions, it is important to focus carefully on the numbers you hear.

🎧 **2** Maria Duran and Peter Flanigan are ready to start playing *Jackpot Shop*. Listen to the program and answer the questions.
- **a.** What prizes did Maria try to win?
- **b.** What prizes did Peter try to win?
- **c.** Who won *Jackpot Shop*?

🎧 **3** Listen to the program again and circle the correct answers.
- **a.** Today's Jackpot Shop is show number _____.
  - 301   341   431
- **b.** Today is Maria's _____ time on the show.
  - 1st   3rd   4th
- **c.** Hernán Cortéz brought chocolate to Europe in _____.
  - 1258   1308   1528
- **d.** Peter and Maria want the combination VCR and color TV with the _____-inch screen.
  - 19   25   29
- **e.** Ray Kroc sold _____ of McDonald's hamburgers before he died.
  - thousands   millions   billions
- **f.** The American Dream car prize is worth _____.
  - $200,000 $2,000,000 $2,000,000,000

Pronunciation

Unstressed *you*

The word *you* is usually unstressed and pronounced **ya** or **/yə/**. Sometimes the **y** sound links with the word before, creating a new sound—**d + y = /dj/** and **t + y = /ch/**.

If you win, what'll you do?   Don't you want to play?
 /yə/   **/yə/** *(reduced)*   **/donchjə/** *(reduced and linked)*

Did you buy the TICKet?
/dɪdjə/ *(reduced and linked)*

4 Predict the pronunciation of *you*. Underline *you* if it is stressed. Put a line through it if it is unstressed.

A: If you hit the jackpot, what'll you do?

B: I don't know. Do you know what you'll do if you win?

A: Of course! I'll go on a cruise to Greece. Do you want to come?

B: I'll tell you what. Let's make a deal. If I win, I'll invite you along, and if you win, you can invite me.

A: It's a deal!

5 Listen to the dialogue and check your answers. With a partner, practice reading the dialogue, focusing on the pronunciation of *you*.

Speak Out

STRATEGY **Describing Consequences** When you want to talk about the possible results or consequences of an action, you can use conditional forms.

If **X** happens, **Y** will happen.   Unless **X** happens, **Y** will/won't happen.
If **X** doesn't happen, **Y** won't happen.

6 Every year the City Club donates money to the group that can best help the city. This year the finalists are the City Opera, the Clean World Club, and the Hospital Helpers.

Work with two other students. Each of you represents a different group. Persuade the other students that your group should get the money.

Example:
A: Well, I think the City Opera deserves the money. If it doesn't get the money, the opera will close for the rest of the year.
B: That's a good cause, but people are more important, and unless the hospital gets that new X-ray machine, patients will not get the quality care they need.

City Opera

The City Opera has been performing in the city for over thirty-five years. Each year they perform fifteen operas. Many important opera stars come to the city to sing. A lot of visitors come to the city to see the operas, too. The tickets are expensive, but the opera also performs for free in high schools and colleges in the city. Every summer they give free performances in the park. If the City Opera does not get the money, it will have to close.

Clean World Club

The Clean World Club is a group of about 200 people who work hard to keep the city clean. The Clean World Club watches the factories to make sure that they do not pollute. It recycles old bottles, cans, and newspapers. It also has a Clean City Day once every month. On these days, the people in the club clean the streets, parks, and rivers. Last year the club also planted over 500 trees. If the club doesn't get the money, it will not be able to do its work.

Hospital Helpers

The Hospital Helpers is a group of about 400 people who buy new machines and furniture for the City Hospital. Last year they built a new emergency room for the hospital. They also bought the hospital over 100 new beds. This year, the hospital needs a new X-ray machine. If the club does not get the money, the hospital will not get the new machine.

READING and WRITING

Read About It

1 **Before You Read** What games did you use to play as a child? What games do you play now? How are they different from the games you used to play?

STRATEGY **Understanding Text Organization** As you read, you will understand more if you look at how writers organize their ideas. One writer may compare two solutions to a problem. Another writer may begin with historical information and then describe recent events. Another writer may classify items. Most writers use a combination of these patterns. Pay attention to how the text is organized.

As you read "Board Games Past and Present," notice how the writer organizes her ideas.

Board Games Past and Present

Board games are a favorite pastime in countries around the world. In fact, board games of different sorts have played an important role in the lives of people since the beginning of time and continue to be important today.

5   In the past, games were related to telling the future, to war, and to funeral ceremonies. For example, in ancient times, people threw animal bones to tell the future. Later, the art of throwing animal bones developed into games with dice. Archaeologists have found board games with dice from as early as 3000 B.C. Other games, such as chess, had their origins in war. In chess, a game that originally came from Iran, the markers represent two armies. The players are the leaders of their
10 armies. In some societies, board games were so important that people left them with the dead. The oldest example of a board game was discovered in a cemetery in Ur, Iraq. Experts think that it dates from 3500 B.C.

    Most board games fall into one of two types, strategy games and chance games. In strategy games, the result of the game depends on the players' skills and abilities.
15 Players must move their markers within rules and think about what the other players are going to do. The player who thinks of the best moves will win. Three strategy games are the Chinese war game Weigi, its Japanese cousin Go, and chess.

    In other games, chance is important. Most of these games are race games. Players move their markers around the board from start to finish. The first player to arrive at
20 the finish is the winner. The results of the game depend on chance—usually the throw of dice. Parcheesi, originally from India, is a chance game that is popular in many countries today.

    Why have games been important in many times
25 and places? Experts say that games let people practice cooperation and competition, two valuable skills. Games also test people's abilities to think. In addition, games are sources of entertainment. For all these reasons, games continue to be a part
30 of our culture.

 Answer the questions.

    a. What were the earliest uses of games?

    b. What are the main kinds of board games?

    c. Why are games still popular today?

 Use the context to guess the meanings of the following words. Write a synonym or short definition. Do not use a dictionary.

    a. ancient (line 5)   **e.** dates from (line 12)

    b. developed (line 6)   **f.** strategy (line 14)

    c. origins (line 8)   **g.** chance (line 18)

    d. leader (line 9)   **h.** depend on (lines 20–21)

Consider the organization of the reading. Circle the letter of the correct answer. In paragraph two, the writer:

a. ranks games from the most difficult to the easiest
b. describes the general history of games
c. lists favorite games

In paragraphs three and four, the writer:

a. criticizes games
b. explains why games are important
c. classifies types of games

Think About It

 What are your favorite games? Are they strategy games or chance games?

Write: Instructions

When you tell someone how to do something, you must write very clear instructions. First, analyze your audience so that you know how much information to present. Then think of all the equipment needed to play and all the steps involved. You also need to define any unfamiliar terms. Finally, organize the steps as they happen, and use transitions to signal the order.

Write About It

7 Think of a simple game you know how to play well. In a paragraph, explain how to play the game. Be sure to give the name of the game, the main objective, and all the materials needed. Then present the rules. Use the example below as a model.

In the game Tic-Tac-Toe, the winner is the person who first gets three Os or three Xs in a straight line. The line can be vertical, horizontal, or diagonal. This game is usually played with pencil and paper. First, a grid of nine squares is drawn. One of two players uses the symbol X and the other player uses the symbol O. The player who goes first decides where he or she wants to mark his or her X or O, and draws it in one of the squares. Next the other player does the same. Then the first player draws an X or O again, then the other player, and so on. Tic-Tac-Toe is a strategy game, so it is important for each player to block the line his or her opponent wants to form while trying to make his or her own line of three symbols in a row.

 8 **Check Your Writing** Exchange papers with a partner. Using the questions below, make suggestions to your partner on ways to make the instructions clearer.

- Are the steps (rules) presented in a logical order?
- Are transitions used to help the reader follow the rules?
- Are unfamiliar terms defined?

1 Complete the conversation with the correct form of the verbs in parentheses. Use the present perfect or present perfect progressive tense.

JANE: Rose, what's wrong? You look worried.

ROSE: I am. I **(1. have)** _____ problems with my son Joey.

JANE: Really? About what?

ROSE: Well, Joey **(2. act)** _____ really different lately. He **(3. lock)** _____ the door to his room and he **(4. play)** _____ his music really loud at night.

JANE: Don't most boys go through that stage?

ROSE: Maybe, but Joey wasn't like that before. And he **(5. be)** _____ so secretive. He **(6. hide)** _____ strange things in his backpack, and **(7. make)** _____ weird noises in his room.

JANE: Well, here he comes now with a package.

ROSE: Hi Joey. What's that?

JOEY: It's a surprise for you, Mom! I **(8. build)** _____ you a birdhouse for your flower garden. I hope you like it!

2 Complete the passage with the correct form of *used to*, *get used to*, or *be used to*.

Jennifer's life is very different from the way it was last year. She **(1.)** _____ live with Hannah, a classmate from school. This year she's living alone. It is hard to adjust, but she **(2.)** _____ being alone in the apartment. She and Hannah **(3.)** _____ spend Sunday mornings eating a long breakfast and reading the paper. Now Jennifer **(4.)** _____ spending Sunday morning eating alone at the neighborhood cafe. One adjustment was easy to make, though. Jennifer **(5.)** _____ the extra closet space right away!

3 Complete the sentences with the correct form of the verbs in parentheses. Some verbs may be negative.

a. If I get in the ticket line early, I **(have)** _____ a better chance of getting concert tickets, don't you think?

b. She **(eat)** _____ her food unless it has a lot of salt on it.

c. If you **(visit)** _____ Barcelona, be sure to see the architecture of Gaudì.

d. You are going to catch a cold if you **(get out of)** _____ those wet clothes.

e. If she **(turn off)** _____ the TV, she'll become a couch potato.

f. If the contestant answers this last question, he **(win)** _____ a trip to Hawaii.

4 Complete each sentence with a verb that makes sense. Use the correct form.

a. If I don't get paid today, I _____ money from my father.

b. We _____ the picnic if it rains.

c. I know Alex _____ you if you ask him politely.

d. Unless the alarm clock _____, I never wake up on time.

e. Jason _____ to the meeting unless we invite him.

f. If Elena _____ the race, she will be very disappointed.

5 Match the sentences with the closest meaning.

1. _____ Max has been looking for a job for six months.

2. _____ Max looked for a job last month.

3. _____ Max hasn't looked for a job yet.

a. Max is not looking for a job anymore.

b. Max is still looking for a job.

c. Max is still studying and will work in the future.

4. _____ Katya used to play the violin.

5. _____ Katya is used to playing the violin.

6. _____ Katya can't get used to playing the violin.

a. Katya practices the violin regularly.

b. Katya has stopped playing the violin.

c. Katya is having trouble playing the violin.

Vocabulary Review

Use the words and expressions in the box to complete the sentences.

afford	origin
thrilled	treasures
wealth	rules
break the record	give me a hand
best seller	fabulous

1. I'm really busy here; I need some help. Could you _____?

2. Now that the Buck family has won the lottery, they can _____ to buy anything they want.

3. When Lucy met Rock N. Roller in person, she was so _____ that she fainted!

4. The game of chess had its _____ in war.

5. My son's goal is to _____ for chewing the most pieces of gum at one time!

6. The _____ of this game are confusing; what do I do next?

7. Examples of some of the world's architectural _____ can be found at the Cloisters museum in New York City.

8. _____ doesn't guarantee happiness, as everybody knows.

9. The *Guinness Book of World Records* is an annual _____.

10. That diamond necklace is worth millions. Isn't it _____?

Base Form	Simple Past	Past Participle
be: am, is, are	was, were	been
become	became	become
begin	began	begun
bend	bent	bent
bite	bit	bitten
blow	blew	blown
break	broke	broken
bring	brought	brought
build	built	built
buy	bought	bought
catch	caught	caught
choose	chose	chosen
come	came	come
cost	cost	cost
cut	cut	cut
do	did	done
draw	drew	drawn
drink	drank	drunk
drive	drove	driven
eat	ate	eaten
fall	fell	fallen
feel	felt	felt
find	found	found
fight	fought	fought
fit	fit	fit
fly	flew	flown
forget	forgot	forgotten
freeze	froze	frozen
get	got	gotten
give	gave	given
go	went	gone
grow	grew	grown
have, has	had	had
hear	heard	heard
hide	hid	hidden
hit	hit	hit
hold	held	held
hurt	hurt	hurt
keep	kept	kept
know	knew	known
leave	left	left

IRREGULAR VERBS

Base Form	Simple Past	Past Participle
lend	lent	lent
lie	lay	lain
lie	lied	lied
light	lit	lit
lose	lost	lost
make	made	made
mean	meant	meant
meet	met	met
pay	paid	paid
put	put	put
quit	quit	quit
read	read	read
ride	rode	ridden
ring	rang	rung
rise	rose	risen
run	ran	run
say	said	said
see	saw	seen
sell	sold	sold
send	sent	sent
set	set	set
sing	sang	sung
sit	sat	sat
sleep	slept	slept
speak	spoke	spoken
speed	sped	sped
spend	spent	spent
stand	stood	stood
steal	stole	stolen
strike	struck	struck
swim	swam	swum
take	took	taken
tell	told	told
think	thought	thought
throw	threw	thrown
understand	understood	understood
wake	woke	woken
wear	wore	worn
win	won	won
write	wrote	written

THE INTERNATIONAL PHONETIC ALPHABET

IPA SYMBOLS

Consonants

/b/	**b**a**b**y, clu**b**	/s/	**s**alt, medi**c**ine, bu**s**
/d/	**d**own, to**d**ay, sa**d**	/š/	**s**ugar, spe**c**ial, fi**sh**
/f/	**f**un, pre**f**er, lau**gh**	/t/	**t**ea, ma**t**erial, da**t**e
/g/	**g**ood, be**g**in, do**g**	/θ/	**th**ing, heal**th**y, ba**th**
/h/	**h**ome, be**h**ind	/ð/	**th**is, mo**th**er, ba**th**e
/k/	**k**ey, cho**c**olate, bla**ck**	/v/	**v**ery, tra**v**el, o**f**
/l/	**l**ate, po**l**ice, mai**l**	/w/	**w**ay, any**o**ne
/m/	**m**ay, wo**m**an, swi**m**	/y/	**y**es, on**i**on
/n/	**n**o, opi**n**ion	/z/	**z**oo, cou**s**in, alway**s**
/ŋ/	a**n**gry, lo**ng**	/ž/	mea**s**ure, gara**g**e
/p/	**p**aper, ma**p**	/č/	**ch**eck, pi**c**ture, wat**ch**
/r/	**r**ain, pa**r**ent, doo**r**	/ǰ/	**j**ob, re**f**ri**g**erator, oran**g**e

Vowels

/ɑ/	**o**n, h**o**t, f**a**ther	/o/	**o**pen, cl**o**se, sh**ow**
/æ/	**a**nd, c**a**sh	/u/	b**oo**t, d**o**, thr**ough**
/ɛ/	**e**gg, s**ay**s, l**ea**ther	/ʌ/	**o**f, y**ou**ng, s**u**n
/ɪ/	**i**n, b**i**g	/ʊ/	p**u**t, c**oo**k, w**ou**ld
/ɔ/	**o**ff, d**augh**ter, dr**aw**	/ə/	**a**bout, penc**i**l, lem**o**n
/e/	**A**pril, tr**ai**n, s**ay**	/ɚ/	moth**er**, Satur**d**ay, doct**or**
/i/	**e**ven, sp**ea**k, tr**ee**	/ɝ/	**ear**th, b**ur**n, h**er**

Diphthongs

/ɑɪ/	**i**ce, st**y**le, l**ie**	/ɔɪ/	**oi**l, n**oi**se, b**oy**
/ɑu/	**ou**t, d**ow**n, h**ow**		

THE ENGLISH ALPHABET

Here is the pronunciation of the letters of the English alphabet, written in International Phonetic Alphabet symbols.

a	/e/	n	/ɛn/
b	/bi/	o	/o/
c	/si/	p	/pi/
d	/di/	q	/kyu/
e	/i/	r	/ɑr/
f	/ɛf/	s	/ɛs/
g	/ǰi/	t	/ti/
h	/eč/	u	/yu/
i	/ɑɪ/	v	/vi/
j	/ǰe/	w	/ˈdʌbəlˌyu/
k	/ke/	x	/ɛks/
l	/ɛl/	y	/wɑɪ/
m	/ɛm/	z	/zi/

UNIT VOCABULARY

STARTING OUT

Nouns
chart
communication
culture
education
experience
hobby
opinion

Verbs
to communicate (with)
to get acquainted (with)
to get down to business
to get to know

UNIT 1

Nouns
cartoon
channel
comedy
commercial
couch potato
detective
documentary
fact
frequency
habit
program
science fiction
soap opera
television guide

Verbs
to participate in
to scan
to turn on
to turn off

Adjectives
bored
favorite
main

Adverbs
almost
ever
generally
how often
normally
once
once in a while
rarely
seldom
twice

UNIT 2

Nouns
band
executive
exercise
film
fortune
gift shop
guard
gym
lobby
nut
privacy
ring
security
snack bar
towel
voice
wig

Verbs
to believe
to come off
to exercise
to film
to follow
to get out of
to hold
to investigate
to lie on
to miss
to practice
to relax
to wait

Adjectives
bald
embarrassing
fantastic
private
public

Adverbs
anymore
still

Expressions
left alone

UNIT 3

Nouns
age
appearance
condition
couple
height
length
location
neighborhood
possession
price
quality
size
speed
truck
weight
yard

Verbs
to compare
to contribute
to purchase
to wonder

Adjectives
attractive
cheap
crowded
enormous
far
gorgeous
huge
jealous
light
low
modern
narrow
perfect
poor
rich
traditional

Expressions
keep up with the Joneses

UNIT 4

Nouns
album
award
compact disc (CD)
entertainment
fan
hit
jazz
opera
prize
record
rock (and roll)
soul
talent
tape
technology

Verbs
to accompany
to appear
to become
to discover
to grow up
to invent
to participate in
to perform
to spread

Adjectives
popular
well-known

Adverbs
finally

UNIT 5

Nouns
accident
alarm
argument
baggage
close call
counter
damage
direction
disaster
earthquake
fire
flood
gate
hurricane
passenger
reaction
storm
tornado

Verbs
to cause
to check in
to damage
to destroy
to get ahead of
to hide
to interrupt
to land (a plane)
to notice
to recover
to rescue
to save (someone)
to scream
to shatter
to shout
to strike
to take off (a plane)

Adjectives
awful
major
minor

Adverbs
as
when
while

Expressions
first of all
in fact

UNIT 6

Nouns
ad
advertisement
advertising
appointment
candy bar
chance
engine
feature
luxury
microwave oven
power
product
soap
wheel

Verbs
to deserve
to own
to persuade
to recommend
to spend

Adjectives
advanced
amazing
comfortable
modern
powerful
up-to-date

Adverbs
right away

Expressions
for example
for instance
namely

UNIT 7

Nouns
application
adventure
candidate
employee
employer
employment
experience
major

prison
popularity
qualification
salary
stunt
success

Verbs
to achieve
to apply

to complain
to fight
to improve
to steal
to take risks

Adjectives
controversial
perfect

qualified
upset

Adverbs
since

Expressions
so far
up to now
in general

UNIT 8

Nouns
advice
credit card
diet
health
hot line
millionaire
pollution
salary

thief
traffic jam

Verbs
to advise
to borrow
to break into
to consult
to gain (weight)
to lose (weight)
to owe

to pay back
to quit
to refuse
to solve
to throw away

Modals
had better
ought to
should

Adjectives
fancy
personal
rapid

Expressions
can't stand

UNIT 9

Nouns
elevator
ingredients
limit
lost and found
pay check
project
stress
technique

Verbs
to calm down
to disappoint
to handle
to keep
to lower
to rank
to remind

Adjectives
anxious
calm
depressed
mental
physical
stressed-out

Expressions
according to
personally
in my opinion
I'd rather

UNIT 10

Nouns
athlete
chemist
collection
contest
encyclopedia
glass
medal
metal
object

record (the best
    done)
reference book
result
spaceship
waste (of time)

Verbs
to break (a record)
to collect

to develop
to give a hand
to exist
to kid
to reach
to set (a record)
to waste

Adjectives
blind
incredible

unbelievable
unusual

Expressions
as a result
for this reason
in addition

UNIT 11

Nouns
adjustment
advantage
appliance
bill
chef
dishwasher
driver's license

Laundromat
laundry
lottery
maid
meal
social life
treasure

Verbs
to adjust
to afford
to be used to
to get used to
to bowl

Adjectives
exhausted
latest

Adverbs
eventually

UNIT 12

Nouns
autobiography
condition
copy
effect
host (of a show)
hostess (of a show)

jackpot
loser
mistake
pastime
player
rule
winner

Verbs
to depend on
to give back
to get along with
to go camping
to hit the jackpot
to make sure

to play
to recycle

Adjectives
fabulous
thrilled

Adverbs
unless

INDEX

Numbers indicate units.